WHEN THE MAN COMES AROUND

CONTENTS

WHEN THE MAN COMES AROUND

A COMMENTARY ON THE BOOK OF REVELATION

DOUGLAS WILSON

canonpress
Moscow, Idaho

Douglas Wilson, *When the Man Comes Around: A Commentary on the Book of Revelation*
Copyright © 2019 by Douglas Wilson

Published by Canon Press
P. O. Box 8729, Moscow, Idaho 83843
800-488-2034 | www.canonpress.com

Cover design by James Engerbretson
Interior design by Valerie Anne Bost
Printed in the United States of America

Library of Congress Cataloging-in-Publication Data
Wilson, Douglas, 1953- author.
When the Man Comes Around: A Commentary on the Book of Revelation / Douglas Wilson.
Moscow, Idaho : Canon Press, 2019.
LCCN 2019011378 | ISBN 9781947644922 (pbk. : alk. paper)
LCSH: Bible. Revelation--Commentaries.
LCC BS2825.53 W57 2019 | DDC 228/.077--dc23
LC record available at https://lccn.loc.gov/2019011378

19 20 21 22 23 24 25 26   10 9 8 7 6 5 4 3 2 1

"Fools Rush In..."

"And though St. John saw many strange
monsters in his vision, he saw no creature so
wild as one of his own commentators."
G.K. Chesterton, *Orthodoxy*

"REVELATION, n. A famous book in which
St. John the Divine concealed all that he
knew. The revealing is done by the commentators, who know nothing."
Ambrose Bierce, *The Devil's Dictionary*

"Blessed is he that readeth, and they that
hear the words of this prophecy, and keep
those things which are written therein: for
the time is at hand."
Revelation 1:3

INTRODUCTION

Now some might say that only a madman would attempt to write a commentary on the book of Revelation. But, having gotten this far, the only thing that remains is to try to brazen it out.

On eschatological subjects, my debts to various writers are too great and numerous, and are spread over too many years, for me to express my gratitude either adequately or accurately. But I would be remiss if I did not mention my obligations to Ken Gentry and Gary DeMar, whose writings on eschatological subjects have been a great help to me over the years.

A different kind of commentary by another writer/editor deserves special mention. Steve Gregg put together a parallel commentary called *Revelation/Four Views*. This was an enormous help to me. There are four basic schools of thought when it comes to interpreting Revelation, and Gregg did the remarkable work of summarizing the views of representatives of all four schools in four parallel columns, all the way through the book of Revelation, passage by passage.

Those four views are historicist, preterist, futurist, and idealist. The outlook represented in this commentary is the preterist, but I was greatly encouraged by how much I learned *from the text* from representatives of all four views. While not sharing the final conclusions of the three other schools, it was a great blessing to still be learning from the same inspired text together.

And I would like to pay this blessing forward. Even if you, the reader, do not come to share my interpretive grid as we work through this vision together, my hope is that we would be able, despite the disagreement, to love the Lord's appearing together. May it not be said of us that the millennium is a thousand years of peace that Christians love to fight about.

Douglas Wilson
Advent 2018

CHAPTER 1

THE SIZE OF HAILSTONES

The Revelation of Jesus Christ, which God gave unto him, to shew unto his servants things which must shortly come to pass; and he sent and signified it by his angel unto his servant John: Who bare record of the word of God, and of the testimony of Jesus Christ, and of all things that he saw. Blessed is he that readeth, and they that hear the words of this prophecy, and keep those things which are written therein: for the time is at hand. (Rev. 1:1–3)

Throughout the book of Revelation, the earth has many plagues that rain down upon it. Over the last two thousand years, Revelation has itself been treated to nearly the same number of interpretations, some of them the size of hailstones. In the course of this study, we will endeavor not to do any of that ourselves, at least not on purpose.

The first thing to note is that the book of Revelation is a revelation, an *unveiling*. It is intended to make things manifest, and so any scheme of interpretation that serves to obscure is an interpretation that should be suspect. This is a *revelation*. Secondly, it is a revelation of Jesus Christ, of and by Him, meaning that any interpretation that leaves Him out of it should also be suspect.

God gave this revelation to Jesus Christ, who in turn signified its truths by His angel, who was sent as a messenger to John, who in his turn showed what was given to the Lord's servants. John gives his account of the Word of God, he testifies to Jesus Christ, and he also narrates for us what he saw. The things he saw are described as things that must *shortly* come to pass (*taxos*—speedily, quickly, swiftly). This means that Revelation is largely concerned with events of the first century. These events were upon them, which John tells us twice. These things must *shortly* take place, and the *time is at hand*. Believing this to be a revelation, and not an obscuring, we should expect the fulfillment of the vast majority of this book to occur within a few years of the time it was given. The operative word is *soon*. With this assumption, many details within the book swim into focus.

John ends his preamble with a blessing. The blessing promised is for those who *read*, those who *hear*, and those who *keep*.

KINGS AND PRIESTS WITH HIM

> John to the seven churches which are in Asia: Grace
> be unto you, and peace, from him which is, and which
> was, and which is to come; and from the seven Spirits
> which are before his throne; And from Jesus Christ,
> who is the faithful witness, and the first begotten of
> the dead, and the prince of the kings of the earth. Unto
> him that loved us, and washed us from our sins in his
> own blood, And hath made us kings and priests unto
> God and his Father; to him be glory and dominion for
> ever and ever. Amen. (Revelation 1:4–6)

John is writing to the seven churches of Asia Minor, modern
day Turkey, and these churches are subsequently named in
chapters two and three of Revelation. They are the churches of Ephesus, Smyrna, Pergamum, Thyatira, Sardis, Philadelphia, and Laodicea. More will be said about each of
them in turn.

The standard Christian blessing at the beginning of a
New Testament letter is "grace and peace." That greeting is used again here—grace to you, John says, and also
peace. Usually, in the other epistles of the New Testament,
the grace and peace are said to be from the Father and
the Son, causing some to wonder why the Holy Spirit is
unmentioned. Jonathan Edwards suggests, and I think he
is correct, that the Spirit is not usually mentioned by name
because the Spirit—proceeding from the Father and the
Son as the Nicene Creed says—is the grace and peace.

Now if that is the case, this expression of it is a significant variation. The grace and peace are cited as being from three sources here, not just two. The first is presumably the Father, the one who "is, and was, and who is to come." Second, there are seven Spirits who are said to be before the Father's throne. The seven may indicate fullness or perfection, or it may be a way of communicating that the grace and peace to the seven churches are from the seven Spirits, that is, the Holy Spirit. And then third, the grace and peace proceed from Jesus Christ, who is identified in three ways. He is the faithful witness (*martyr*), He is the firstborn from the dead, and He is the prince (*archon*) of the kings of the earth.

In pondering the meaning of the seven Spirits, it is worth remembering what Isaiah says. "And there shall come forth a rod out of the stem of Jesse, And a Branch shall grow out of his roots: And the spirit of the Lord shall rest upon him, The spirit of wisdom and understanding, The spirit of counsel and might, The spirit of knowledge and of the fear of the Lord" (Isaiah 11:1–2).

The Messiah will come, and the Spirit of the Lord will rest upon Him (one). The Spirit of wisdom and understanding (two more). The Spirit of counsel and might (two more). And then we have the Spirit of the knowledge and of the fear of the Lord (two more). Seven in all.

A doxological blessing is then declared concerning Jesus Christ. "Unto Him who loved us . . ." He is the one who loved us and He is the one who washed us from our sins in His own blood. The verb for *washing* here is striking and clear. The image used by hymn writers—that of being washed in the blood of Christ—is therefore a biblical image. This is the same one who, after that cleansing, made us kings and priests together with Him. He is the one who should consequently receive glory and dominion forever. And an *Amen* is added to it.

THE CORONATION OF CHRIST

> Behold, he cometh with clouds; and every eye shall see
> him, and they also which pierced him: and all kindreds
> of the earth shall wail because of him. Even so, Amen.
> I am Alpha and Omega, the beginning and the ending,
> saith the Lord, which is, and which was, and which is
> to come, the Almighty. (Rev. 1:7–8).

This is a good place to note that Revelation is simply saturated with citations from the Old Testament. This short passage takes material from at least two places, and those places help throw light on what John is talking about here. "Coming on the clouds" is from Daniel 7:13, and looking on Him whom "they have pierced" is from Zechariah 12:10.

In Daniel, the coming on clouds is not the Second Coming, but is rather the coming of the glorified Son of Man into the throne room of the Ancient of Days. It is a reference to the Ascension, not to the Second Coming. John has just finished telling us that Jesus is the *archon* of the kings of the earth, which is what happened at the Ascension. When Jesus approached the Ancient of Days, He was given full and complete authority, dominion, and glory. He was given a kingdom such that all people, nations, and languages should serve Him—in short, everlasting dominion.

The Ascension was His coronation as *archon* of the kings of the earth. Revelation is a description of how He began that reign two thousand years ago, and how His reign would culminate at the end of all history in the appearance of the bride from Heaven.

In Zechariah, the prophet describes a day in which the people will see the one they pierced, and how they will mourn for Him. That day is described as a day in which the Spirit of Grace and Supplication is "poured" upon the house of David and upon the inhabitants of Jerusalem. This is a description of Pentecost—when the Spirit was literally poured out upon them—in that city, to that extent, and with that effect.

We are enabled to see the Lord's approach to the Ancient of Days through the preaching of the gospel. This is what it means to declare the Lordship of Jesus Christ. We are enabled to see Him as pierced through the preaching of the gospel. This is what it means to portray Him as crucified. We are enabled to mourn for our sins through the preaching of the gospel. This is what it means when the one who was pierced pierces our hearts. As John says, even so, and Amen.

We do not need to marvel at how such things can be accomplished through the folly of preaching because the heart of the message preached is a Person. He is the first and last, the height and the depth, the Alpha and Omega, the one in whom we live and move and have our being. It is appropriate that He was given everything by the Ancient of Days because He Himself is the one who is, who was, and who is to come. Before Abraham was, I am, He said.

THREE-FOLD FELLOWSHIP

> I John, who also am your brother, and companion in
> tribulation, and in the kingdom and patience of Jesus
> Christ, was in the isle that is called Patmos, for the
> word of God, and for the testimony of Jesus Christ.
> (Rev. 1:9)

The writer identifies himself simply as John. He is tradi-
tionally taken as John the apostle, and for good reason.
Although Revelation is a completely different genre from
the gospels, the close kinship between this book and the
fourth gospel is plain.

He describes himself two ways. The first is simply as
"brother." The second is "companion," a rendering of *syn-
koinonos*—a "partaker together with." The apostle is a
brother together with those to whom he is writing, and
he also fellowships together with them, partaking together
with them, in three things. The first bond of their fellowship is tribulation, the second is the kingdom, and the third
is perseverance. All three are connected to Jesus Christ—
they are the tribulation of Jesus, the kingdom of Jesus, and
the endurance of Jesus.

John was on the isle of Patmos—a small Greek island in
the Aegean. He was exiled there, as he says, "for the word
of God" and because of his "testimony of Jesus Christ."
The word for testimony is *marturia*, which is related to our
word *martyr*. A martyr is one who witnesses or testifies to
what he has seen or experienced. Because faithful martyrs
have often had to seal their testimony with their blood, the

word has come to mean one who dies for his faith, as Antipas did (Rev. 2:13). But the witness who is willing to go to the point of death begins witnessing a lot earlier than that in the course of his life. The spirit of prophecy is the testimony of Jesus (Rev. 19:10). John was exiled to Patmos for the testimony of Jesus Christ, and while he was there, he was given the Revelation of Jesus Christ.

IN THE SPIRIT ON THE LORD'S DAY

> I was in the Spirit on the Lord's day, and heard behind me a great voice, as of a trumpet, Saying, I am Alpha and Omega, the first and the last: and, What thou seest, write in a book, and send it unto the seven churches which are in Asia; unto Ephesus, and unto Smyrna, and unto Pergamos, and unto Thyatira, and unto Sardis, and unto Philadelphia, and unto Laodicea. (Revelation 1:10–11)

John begins to tell us the beginning of the vision. He had been exiled to Patmos, and on a particular Lord's Day, he was in the Spirit. This tells us, incidentally, that there is a day set apart for the Lord, the first day of the week, the day He rose from the dead, which is to say, Sunday. John was in the Spirit, which is to say he was in a trance, capable of seeing the vision that he saw.

While in that condition, he heard a great voice behind him and he turned and looked. This is a something we see later in Revelation. He first hears, then turns, and looks at what he heard (Rev. 7: 4, 9). The speaker behind him had a great voice, clear as a trumpet, and He identified Himself as Jesus Christ. The way He did this was by calling Himself the Alpha and Omega (the first and last letters in the Greek alphabet), and then repeating it another way by saying He was the first and the last.

John is then given his commission—he is told to write down in a book what he sees in the vision, and then he is to send that book to the seven church in the province of Asia. Those seven churches, in order, were Ephesus, Smyrna, Pergamos, Thyatira, Sardis, Philadelphia, and Laodicea.

IN OUR MIDST

> And I turned to see the voice that spake with me. And being turned, I saw seven golden candlesticks; And in the midst of the seven candlesticks one like unto the Son of Man, clothed with a garment down to the foot, and girt about the paps with a golden girdle. (Rev. 1:12–13)

John has heard a loud voice, a voice like a trumpet. He turns to see who is speaking, and the speaker is obliquely identified as the Lord Jesus. The first thing John saw was the collection of lampstands. These lampstands are identified just a few verses down as the seven churches of Asia to which John is writing (v. 20). This vision of the Lord includes a number of vivid descriptions that run into the next verses, which we will get to shortly, but for now it should simply be said that the one who spoke, telling John to write to the seven churches, was the Lord Himself. He is identified as one "like a Son of Man," which is how the Messiah is described in Daniel 7:13 when He was presented before the Ancient of Days and was given universal dominion (Dan. 7:14).

The thing that should be emphasized here is that the seven lampstands are the seven churches, and the Lord was standing in the midst of the churches. He identifies with them, He stands with them, and as we shall see, He holds their pastors in His right hand (v. 16). He walks among them.

A VOICE LIKE MANY WATERS

> His head and his hairs were white like wool, as white as snow; and his eyes were as a flame of fire; And his feet like unto fine brass, as if they burned in a furnace; and his voice as the sound of many waters. (Rev. 1:14–15)

A vivid description is given of the Lord Jesus, and in true apocalyptic colors. He wore a long robe, down to the feet. The color of the robe is not specified here, but He had a golden sash around His chest. Both His head and hair were white, strikingly white—white like wool, white like snow. His eyes were fiery flames, and His feet were like refined brass just out of the furnace. His voice was like the sound of many waters.

The golden girdle around His chest indicates priesthood (Ex. 28:8), although the Lord Jesus held a priesthood much higher than that of Aaron. His head and hair were white, not like the whiteness of skin, but a pure white. In the next verse (v. 16), we see that His face shone like the sun at full strength, so it was a penetrating whiteness. Picture a sun that is white, not yellow. Feet that are like burnished bronze also show up in the Old Testament—the feet of the cherubim that surrounded the throne of God had feet that color (Ezek. 1:7). And the angelic messenger that came to Daniel was very much like this (Dan. 10:6) in a number of particulars. His face was like lightning, his eyes like torches, his feet like burnished bronze, and his voice was like many waters. John is clearly describing the Lord with terms previously used for one of His great servants.

Having a voice like many waters is not an unusual scriptural trope. "And, behold, the glory of the God of Israel came from the way of the east: and his voice was like a noise of many waters: and the earth shined with his glory" (Ezek. 43:2). Such a voice sounds like thunder (Rev. 14:2), and later on John says that it sounded like a huge multitude, or a great thundering (Rev. 19:6). When we open our Bibles to read the Word of God, or attend worship in order to hear it declared, we should feel like we are standing on a rocky beach near the base of Niagara Falls. God's Word fills all the available space.

A PROFOUND MYSTERY

> And he had in his right hand seven stars: and out of his mouth went a sharp twoedged sword: and his countenance was as the sun shineth in his strength. (Rev. 1:16)

The description of Jesus Christ continues in the same vein. Here we learn three more things about Him—that Jesus holds seven stars in His right hand, a sharp two-edged sword comes out of His mouth, and His face shines like the sun in its full strength.

The messengers of the churches, their angels, are described under the figure of stars in the Lord's right hand. The image is one of the Lord's presence with those churches—the lampstands are the churches, and the stars are therefore their pastors (v. 20). If the "angels" were *heavenly* emissaries, this would be an odd way to describe them. The entire scenario portrays the Lord's identification with the churches, and in this case, with their pastors. The pastors are stars, and this is said to be a "mystery."

This ties in with the next description. The word *angel* simply means "messenger." It is used (of course) of heavenly messengers, but it is also a word that describes human messengers. For example, John the Baptist is said to be an angel (Mark 1:2), and these angels are also men assigned to the churches. But as messengers, they do not have the authority to come up with their own messages. They do not speak on their own authority. They are heralds, men commissioned to announce what someone else has told them to say.

And this is how they are pictured here. Jesus is the one speaking. When Christ speaks to the churches, the double-edge sword comes out of His mouth, and His ministers are held in His right hand as He preaches. This is what gospel authority means. Jesus speaks the Word while He holds the men speaking it. A few verses later, the pastor at Pergamos is told that this is where his authority lies—"to the angel of the church in Pergamos write: These things saith he which hath the sharp sword with two edges" (Rev. 2:12).

Later in Revelation the two-edged sword (representing preaching) is associated with the rod of iron which Christ will use to rule the nations (Rev. 19:15). This rod of iron is prophesied in Psalm 2:9, and the Lord wields it through His servants (Rev. 2:26-27), but the Lord Himself is the one who holds it (Rev. 12:5).

The Bridal City is described later as having no need for a sun because her Bridegroom is that sun (Rev. 21:23; 22:5). That reality as later described is foreshadowed here.

THE KEYS OF DEATH AND HADES

> And when I saw him, I fell at his feet as dead. And he
> laid his right hand upon me, saying unto me, Fear not;
> I am the first and the last: I am he that liveth, and was
> dead; and, behold, I am alive for evermore, Amen; and
> I have the keys of hell and of death. (Rev. 1:17–18)

Understandably, when John saw this vision, he simply collapsed. The vision was overpowering, and John fell down, virtually dead. But the Lord—for He here clearly identifies Himself as the Lord Jesus—laid His right hand on John. This is the same right hand that holds the seven stars, who are the pastors of the seven churches in Asia. When the Lord touched John with His right hand, His first words were "fear not." The vision preceding provided ample reasons for collapsing, but the words that follow were the Lord's encouragement to rise up and "write." The vision was overwhelming; the words were enabling.

The reasons for gathering himself together were these. Jesus is the first and the last. He is the one who was alive,

died, and who rose again from the dead to live for-
.r. This was sealed with a solemn Amen. In addition to
.verything else, the Lord Jesus—on account of His descent
into Hades and His resurrection from that place—was the
possessor of the keys of both death and Hades.

The word rendered as *hell* in the AV is actually Hades. This
is not *Gehenna*, the place of final condemnation, but rather
Sheol/Hades, the place of the dead where Jesus preached
to the disobedient souls from Noah's era (1 Pet. 3:19-20).
Jesus is now the Lord of death, the conqueror of Hades.

WHAT WILL HAPPEN NEXT

> Write the things which thou hast seen, and the things
> which are, and the things which shall be hereafter;
> (Rev. 1:19)

John is then instructed to write down what he has seen.
Revelation has many "time stamps" within it, but it also
has some time hints, like this one. John is told to write
what he has seen, the things that are happening in the
present, and the things that will occur after that, in the
future. He is not told to write down what has happened,
what is happening right then, and then to hit the pause
button for two thousand years or more. The expectation
clearly is that the "things hereafter" are the things that will
be unfolding in the immediate future.

This is supported by the time stamps that occur elsewhere in the book. Two thousand years ago, the things
described in this book were going to happen *soon* (Rev.
1:1). The Lord was coming *soon* (Rev. 3:1). The Christians

of that era were warned about what must *soon* take place (Rev. 22:6). The Lord was indeed going to come and fulfill His words *soon* (Rev. 22:7, 12, 20).

This same reality is assumed in this passage. Write down what you have seen, what you are seeing, and what you will see (right after this).

WHY THE ANGELS SPEAK

> The mystery of the seven stars which thou sawest in my right hand, and the seven golden candlesticks. The seven stars are the angels of the seven churches: and the seven candlesticks which thou sawest are the seven churches. (Rev. 1:20)

The last verse of this chapter may be considered the introduction to the next two chapters. In this section of Revelation that is opening up, messages are being given to the angels of the seven churches of Asia. Remember the Lord Jesus was standing in the midst of seven lampstands (Rev. 1:12-13), He held seven stars in His right hand (Rev. 1:16), and a sharp two-edged sword came out of His mouth. In this verse, we are given the meaning of the mystery, and in the two chapters to come, we will see how the Lord exercises this ministry.

So we know that the seven lampstands are the seven churches and that the Lord Jesus was walking around in the midst of His churches. The seven stars that He held in His right hand are the seven "messengers," or pastors of these churches. The sword in His mouth is His Word, which He gives to the successive pastors in the upcoming passages.

So this is how it works: Jesus speaks, and then He tells John to write what He has spoken. The implication is that the angel of the church is to speak what he has read. So Jesus speaks, John writes, the angel reads, and the angel speaks.

CHAPTER 2

MEN WHO WERE SENT

> Unto the angel of the church of Ephesus write; These
> things saith he that holdeth the seven stars in his right
> hand, who walketh in the midst of the seven golden
> candlesticks; (Rev. 2:1)

We have come to the introduction of the passage where
the Lord speaks to all seven churches through their appointed angels or "messengers." He has a word to speak to
the church at Ephesus, and so he writes to the "messenger"
of that church. The message to the angel and the message
to the church are identical. God speaks to His churches
through His appointed and ordained servants.

The word *angel* need not refer to what we would call an angelic or celestial being. John the Baptist was called an angel (Mark 1:2). Human beings are called angels in the Old Testament also (Job 1:14; Is. 42:19; Mal. 2:7; 3:1). And the word is used by Luke to refer to ordinary messengers. Jesus "sent messengers (angels) before his face: and they went, and entered into a village of the Samaritans, to make ready for him" (Luke 9:52; cf. 7:24). Now of course it is possible that the angels of the first chapters of Revelation are celestial beings, but in my view this creates many more problems than it solves.

So in the preamble to the message to the pastor of the Ephesian church, the Lord reminds him of the context. That man is not receiving a private word, or a private revelation. This comes from the one who holds seven stars in His right hand, and as He is speaking to one of them, the reminder is that there are six other messengers there with the pastor. The Lord who speaks this admonition to Ephesus is the same Lord who is walking in the midst of seven lampstands. The Lord ministers, in other words, within a community of churches.

What He says to each, He says pointedly to each, but all of them are invited to take warning from what he says to each. The Lord is praising and admonishing these churches in public. The saints in Laodicea and Philadelphia will know what was said to Ephesus, and vice versa.

THE MISSING ELEMENT

I know thy works, and thy labour, and thy patience, and how thou canst not bear them which are evil: and

thou hast tried them which say they are apostles, and
are not, and hast found them liars: And hast borne,
and hast patience, and for my name's sake hast la-
boured, and hast not fainted. (Rev. 2:2–3)

In many ways, the church at Ephesus had their act together. When the Lord begins to speak to them directly, he
commends them heartily at first. This was the church that
had received the magnificent epistle to the Ephesians, and
the apostle Paul had labored there in Ephesus for a few
years. They had internalized the teaching, and they were
faithful in their defense of it.

The Lord commends their works, their labor, and their
patience. Another item of praise, and one that modern
churches need to pay close attention to, is the fact that
Jesus praised the intolerance of the Ephesian church. They
could not bear those who were evil. They tested certain
false apostles and found them to be false.

They were a hard-working church. They had to bear a
great deal for the sake of the Lord's name, and they did so
with patience. They persevered in this labor and did not
give up.

But that does not mean all was well. Their works were
sound, but something was missing, and that threatened to
ruin all.

LIFE IN THE MIDST

Nevertheless I have somewhat against thee, because
thou hast left thy first love. Remember therefore from
whence thou art fallen, and repent, and do the first

works; or else I will come unto thee quickly, and will
remove thy candlestick out of his place, except thou
repent. But this thou hast, that thou hatest the deeds
of the Nicolaitans, which I also hate. He that hath an
ear, let him hear what the Spirit saith unto the churches; To him that overcometh will I give to eat of the tree
of life, which is in the midst of the paradise of God.
(Rev. 2:4–7)

This pointed admonition to the Ephesian church is filled
with balanced tensions. The message began by praising
them for their *works,* but rapidly comes to the point of
urging them to return to the *works* they did at first. He tells
them here that they have abandoned their first love. The
word translated *abandon* admits of numerous legitimate
translations. I think one of them that makes good sense of
the context is that they had *grown slack* in their first love.
Combine this with the word he uses to remind them where
they had *fallen* from. Given this description, and that lack
of repentance would result in the lampstand of the church
being removed and the extinction of the Ephesian church,
we see that the situation was very grave.

Their love was seriously unhealthy—but their hatred was
still sound. The Lord commends them for that. They hated
the works of the Nicolaitans, which the Lord also hated.
We don't know who these followers of Nicolas were, or
what their works consisted of, but we do know they were
hateful. Their works contrasted poorly with the works that
are commended in the Ephesians, and to which the Ephesians were summoned to return. The dismaying condition

of the church at Ephesus was found in the fact that they were orthodox in their hatred, but not in their love.

The one who had an ear to listen was invited to listen. True listening means obeying and returning to the works that were powered by their first love. This is what it means to overcome. And the one who overcomes will be given fruit from the tree of life, located in the midst of the paradise of God. Paradise is defined here as being where the tree of life is. We see later in the book that the tree of life is located inside the new Jerusalem, which is the bride, the wife of the Lamb, the Christian church (Rev. 22:2, 14). The tree of life is in the *midst* (*mesos*) of the paradise of God. The Lord Jesus walks in the midst of the lampstands (Rev. 1: 13; 2:1). The tree of life is where the Lord Jesus is.

POVERTY CAMOUFLAGE

> And unto the angel of the church in Smyrna write; These things saith the first and the last, which was dead, and is alive; I know thy works, and tribulation, and poverty, (but thou art rich) and I know the blasphemy of them which say they are Jews, and are not, but are the synagogue of Satan. (Rev. 2:8–9)

The second message is delivered to Smyrna, a city about fifty miles north of Ephesus. Remember that John is on Patmos, an island to the southwest of Ephesus about sixty-three miles away.

The Lord Jesus identifies Himself here in two different ways. The first is by saying He is the first and the last, the *protos* and *eschatos*, the beginning and the end. He encompasses all of human history; He contains it all. Not only does He contain all human history, but He established Himself as Lord in the very middle of it by His resurrection from the dead. He identifies Himself as the one "which was dead, and is alive."

We will see in chapter three that Smyrna provides a sharp contrast with Laodicea. Laodicea has a name for being rich, but is actually poor. Smyrna goes the other way. The Lord knows their poverty, but adds that they are actually rich. The Lord knows their works, their trials, and how they have camouflaged their spiritual wealth with poverty.

The saints at Smyrna also had to contend with false Jews who were guilty of blasphemy. The word *blasphemy* has two basic senses: One means railing against God, saying vile things about Him, and the other is slanderous accusation against God's people. Given the context here, the blasphemy was probably directed against the church at Smyrna by Jewish persecutors. But John goes on to add that such people claim to be Jews, but are not. They are actually members of the synagogue of Satan, whose name means *adversary*.

FAITHFUL TO DEATH

> Fear none of those things which thou shalt suffer: behold, the devil shall cast some of you into prison, that ye may be tried; and ye shall have tribulation ten days: be thou faithful unto death, and I will give thee a crown of life. He that hath an ear, let him hear what

the Spirit saith unto the churches; He that overcometh
shall not be hurt of the second death. (Rev. 2:10–11)

The church at Smyrna was standing at the edge of persecution. The Lord encourages them in that place by telling
them not to fear what they are about to suffer. This implies
two things. One is that they will in fact suffer, and the
other is that in Christ they have no need to fear. The specific persecution they faced was going to be stirred up by the
devil. Some of them would be thrown into prison so that
they might be tried or tested. The tribulation would last for
ten days. We can assume that it was going to end in death
for some of them, because the Lord promises the crown of
life for those who would be faithful to the point of death.

The one who has an ear should take heed and hear. This
is what the Spirit is saying to the churches (plural). The
second death is something that should be feared, and those
who are faithful through the first death need not fear it.

We do not have any extra-biblical record of a persecution there lasting for ten days, but there is no real reason
we should. Because this persecution is said to come from
the devil, and the unbelieving Jews were identified as a
synagogue of Satan, it is likely that this would be a persecution arising from these unbelieving Jews.

DWELLING WHERE SATAN DWELT

And to the angel of the church in Pergamos write;
These things saith he which hath the sharp sword with
two edges; I know thy works, and where thou dwellest, even where Satan's seat is: and thou holdest fast

> my name, and hast not denied my faith, even in those
> days wherein Antipas was my faithful martyr, who
> was slain among you, where Satan dwelleth. (Rev.
> 2:12–13)

The church at Pergamum was a church that was already experiencing persecution. In the course of these letters, the Lord has been warning all the believers in Asia Minor of this impending reality, but in some places it had already begun. Pergamum was one of those places. John says that "Satan's seat" was there, which is likely a reference to emperor worship. Even though the emperor was in Rome, the most organized location for emperor worship was in Asia Minor, where these seven churches were. The cult of Rome had been planted in Pergamum as early as 29 B.C. and there was no quicker way for the Christians to prove their lack of patriotism than to refuse to go along with worship of the emperor.

The church there was characterized by a faithful witness in the face of hostility, and John mentions one martyr by name, Antipas. The church was characterized by the same faithfulness that Antipas had shown. This was a sound church, a faithful church.

There are two striking things about these words of exhortation. The first is that Satan is mentioned *twice*. He had his seat there, and he made his dwelling there. But the same thing is said about the believers there. John says that they dwelt where Satan's seat was, and that Satan dwelt there. In other words, these faithful Christians dwelt where Satan dwelt, and hence the conflict.

The other striking thing is that both sides are armed. We don't know how Antipas died, but we know his blood was shed. He was killed. But how were the Christians armed? In his address to this persecuted church, Jesus is described as the one who had the sharp, double-edged sword. In the earlier vision we saw that this sword came out of His mouth. That meant that the pagans would fight with material swords, and the Christians would fight with the sword of Christ, the Word of God.

JESUS PROMISES TO FIGHT THE CHRISTIANS

> But I have a few things against thee, because thou hast there them that hold the doctrine of Balaam, who taught Balac to cast a stumblingblock before the children of Israel, to eat things sacrificed unto idols, and to commit fornication. So hast thou also them that hold the doctrine of the Nicolaitans, which thing I hate. Repent; or else I will come unto thee quickly, and will fight against them with the sword of my mouth. (Revelation 2:14–16)

The church at Pergamum had done well against the hostility of overt persecution. Even when Antipas was killed, they stood firm. But that does not mean that the church was above criticism. The Lord had a few things against them, and it pertained to what they were willing to tolerate in their midst. We know the content of the false teaching that had some presence there, but there are two ways to read what we call it.

The Ephesian church had a commendation from the Lord in that he hated the deeds of a group called the Nicolaitans. In Pergamum, their problems was that they tolerated this same group. Now here are the two ways to read it. One would say that Pergamum had a problem with two false groups in her midst—those who followed the teaching of Balaam, and those who followed the teaching of the Nicolaitans (whatever that was). In spite of much speculation, we don't know the particular sin of this group. The other possibility is that the Nicolaitans were in fact the group that was promulgating the error of Balaam. That is how I am reading it here.

Balaam was not a Hebrew, but his prophetic gift was genuine. In the Old Testament outline of the story, Balaam was hired to curse the Israelites, which he refused to do. But there are hints that he then took Balak aside and gave him some "off-the-record" counsel on how to use their women as a weapon against Israel. This advice was taken, and for a limited time was very successful. The New Testament is more explicit about Balaam's sin in this than is the Old, and this is one of the places. Balaam "taught" Balak what to do, and it was a way of luring the Israelites into idolatry by means of fornication. The women of Moab offered themselves as bait, and so Israel sinned at Baalpeor (Numbers 25:3).

The church at Pergamum had some people there who were of the party of the Nicolaitans, who were essentially offering the same thing. The Lord declares that this is something that He hates. He summons the church at Pergamum to repent of their tolerance. If they do not repent,

He will come to them "quickly," and He will fight against them with the sword of His mouth. Notice that the Word of Christ, the double-edged sword that comes from the mouth of Christ, is a weapon that is deployed against a Christian church that has lapsed into a tolerance of sexual immorality. The word translated as fight here is *polemeo*, the word from which we get polemics. Jesus promises to fight the Christians.

THE WHITE STONE

> He that hath an ear, let him hear what the Spirit saith unto the churches; To him that overcometh will I give to eat of the hidden manna, and will give him a white stone, and in the stone a new name written, which no man knoweth saving he that receiveth it. (Rev. 2:17)

The letter to the church at Pergamum concludes with one of the most personal individual exhortations in the Scriptures. The general invitation is given: Whoever has an ear, let him hear what the Spirit is saying to the churches. The Spirit speaks to the churches corporately, and all Christians are invited individually to hear. To the one who overcomes—which is to say, to the one who is born anew, regenerate, born again—God promises to give him hidden manna. "For whatsoever is born of God overcometh the world: and this is the victory that overcometh the world, even our faith" (1 John 5:4). The victory that overcomes the world is our faith, and it is by faith that we receive the free grace of justification. The only one to whom this happens is the one who is born of God. If a man is born of God, then he overcomes the world. If a man is born of God, then he receives hidden manna.

What a curious phrase. In order to be manna at all, it must come from heaven. But the manna in the wilderness fell on all Israel—those with true faith and those with no faith could see it equally. But to the one who is regenerate, God gives hidden manna, manna that only he knows about. This hidden manna is Christ Himself. "This is that bread which came down from heaven: not as your fathers did eat manna, and are dead: he that eateth of this bread shall live for ever" (John 6:58). Mark it well—you are not saved without the hidden Christ.

This glorious truth is then given under another image, but an image that was closely related. "And the manna was as coriander seed, and the colour thereof as the colour of bdellium" (Numbers 11:7). Bdellium was an aromatic resin, but it may also have been the name of a precious stone (Gen. 2:12). Manna was the color of bdellium, which was apparently white. If so, this is likely the white stone that is referenced here. And here is where the true individual consolation comes in. To the one who overcomes, to the one who is born again, God gives the hidden Christ and a new name that only God and the beloved saint know. But God gives no new name unless He has first given a new heart.

A MESSENGER

And unto the angel of the church in Thyatira write; These things saith the Son of God, who hath his eyes

like unto a flame of fire, and his feet are like fine brass.
(Rev. 2:18)

Thyatira was about 128 miles from Patmos, where John
was exiled as he wrote these exhortations to the cities.
What he wrote was delivered as a circular. From Ephesus, you would work northward toward Smyrna, and from
there to Pergamum. At Pergamum, the route would turn
east and head toward Thyatira. After Thyatira, the course
would run southeast through Sardis, Philadelphia and Laodicea. All the churches, and Patmos also, could fit inside
a circle with a radius of about 86 miles.

The city was not a great sophisticated city, but rather
a working town, home to manufacturing and commercial
guilds. Lydia was a merchant in purple goods, and although she was converted in Philippi, she was from Thyatira (Acts 16:14).

His feet were like fine brass, which is how the feet of
the four living creatures in Ezekiel are described. Their
feet were the color of burnished brass (Ez. 1:7). This language is particularly taken from the vision of the angel that
Daniel saw (Dan. 10:5-6). The man there clothed in linen
is like the vision of Christ in this place in two respects. In
both places the eyes are described as flames or lamps of
fire, and the feet are described as brass.

Apart from anything else the imagery might mean, it
certainly means that the messenger is from God, and that
his words must be obeyed.

JEZEBEL IN YOUR CHURCH

> I know thy works, and charity, and service, and faith, and thy patience, and thy works; and the last to be more than the first. Notwithstanding I have a few things against thee, because thou sufferest that woman Jezebel, which calleth herself a prophetess, to teach and to seduce my servants to commit fornication, and to eat things sacrificed unto idols. (Rev. 2:19–20)

The church at Thyatira was an industrious, hard-working church. In speaking to them, the Lord begins by commending them for their labors. He uses a number of overlapping terms to do so—He praises their works, using that word twice, once at the beginning and the other at the end of the list. He commends their works, and then their love, and their faith, and their steadfastness, and then their works again. The works at the end of the list were greater than the works at the beginning. Their labors were growing in volume and intensity. The church at Ephesus worked hard also, but had fallen from their first love. The church at Thyatira was given over to ever-increasing works, but they were also commended for their love (*agape*). All in all, they appeared to be a healthy church.

But there was a problem. A woman who was a false teacher, styling herself as a prophetess, was seducing servants of Christ (the Lord calls them *my* servants) into fornication, and into participation in idolatrous feasts. She was here given the pseudonym of Jezebel, after the Phoenician queen who introduced Baal worship into Israel in the time of Elijah. The charge against the church at Thyatira was that they *tolerated* her.

THE SIN IS THE PUNISHMENT

> And I gave her space to repent of her fornication; and she repented not. Behold, I will cast her into a bed, and them that commit adultery with her into great tribulation, except they repent of their deeds. And I will kill her children with death; and all the churches shall know that I am he which searcheth the reins and hearts: and I will give unto every one of you according to your works. (Rev. 2:21–23)

Jezebel was a false prophetess who made room for sexual license among her disciples, a doctrine that is too often an easy sell. She was a professing Christian and was part of the church there in Thyatira. The Lord's judgments are not always immediate. In this case, He had given her a warning, and time to repent of her fornication. But she did not take advantage of the opportunity, and refused to repent.

Sexual immorality is not just a sin for which there will be judgment later. It is a sin which is in itself a judgment. The sin incurs a judgment, and the sin is a judgment. In Romans 1, it is the wrath of God that gives men up to unrighteous desires. "The mouth of strange women is a deep pit: He that is abhorred of the LORD shall fall therein" (Prov. 22:14). We find something similar here. Those who commit adultery with Jezebel will together with her be pitched into "great tribulation"—unless of course they repent. They will suffer greatly, and Jezebel's children will die. But note that all these consequences for the adultery (which are judgments) are the result of what happened in the bed of adultery—and it was the *Lord* who cast her into that bed.

The Lord is the one who judges the heart, as we would put it. In the Authorized Version it says that God searches "the reins and hearts." This is a reflection of the Greek original. Reins refers to the kidneys—which, according to the ancient Hebrew metaphor, referred to the innermost part of a man. God sees all our actions, all the way to the bottom layer, and He is the one who judges us according to our works.

SINFUL TOLERATION

> But unto you I say, and unto the rest in Thyatira, as many as have not this doctrine, and which have not known the depths of Satan, as they speak; I will put upon you none other burden. But that which ye have already hold fast till I come. (Rev. 2:24–25)

Jezebel was tolerated in Thyatira, and this was a big problem. It was a problem for her and for her followers because they were going to be chastised by the Lord directly. It was a problem for the leadership at Thyatira because they were the ones who put up with this contagion in the church. The Lord promises to parse the situation out, in accordance with the works of "each one of you."

The next word is a bit more encouraging. The toleration of Jezebel was a problem, but the Lord continues to talk to the church leadership (apparently) along with the rest of the saints in Thyatira, the ones who had not been corrupted with this licentious teaching. It is interesting to note how John references how these false teachers described their own teaching—as "the depths of Satan." They were apparently peddling some sort of deep heavy, and the Lord will have none of it.

He says that He will put no additional burden on them. I take this to mean that there is no additional task beyond the implied task of no longer tolerating Jezebel. No additional labor is necessary. Get rid of that woman, and hold on tight until the Lord relieves you.

THE REWARD OF PERSEVERING

> And he that overcometh, and keepeth my works unto the end, to him will I give power over the nations: And he shall rule them with a rod of iron; as the vessels of a potter shall they be broken to shivers: even as I received of my Father. And I will give him the morning star. He that hath an ear, let him hear what the Spirit saith unto the churches. (Rev. 2:26–29)

The church at Thyatira was having trouble keeping the corruption of the nations out of the church. But the Lord calls them to faithfulness, and urges them to overcome and keep His works to the end. For the believer who does that, God will give him authority (*exousia*) over the nations. In short, exercising dominion within the church, according to the Word, will result in dominion in the world. In the second psalm, God promises that the Christ will be given a rod of iron to rule over the nations, and here the Christ promises that the overcomer will share in that rule with

Him. As the Christ received authority from the Father, so also will the servants of Christ receive authority from Him—and it is all at the root the same authority. That rule is not all sunshine—the nations are sometimes shattered in the process. Jesus came, after all, to set the world on fire (Luke 12:49). To the one who overcomes, God will give him the morning star. This is simply the gift of Christ under another figure. Christ is the morning star (Rev. 22:16). The one who is able to hear needs to make a point of hearing what the Spirit says to all the churches.

CHAPTER 3

STRENGTHEN WHAT IS LEFT

> And unto the angel of the church in Sardis write; These
> things saith he that hath the seven Spirits of God, and
> the seven stars; I know thy works, that thou hast a
> name that thou livest, and art dead. Be watchful, and
> strengthen the things which remain, that are ready to
> die: for I have not found thy works perfect before God.
> (Rev. 3:1–2)

Sardis was in the region of Lydia in Asia Minor, and was
the regional capital. It is the next church of the seven, and
according to the message they received, it was in a dire condition. The church was apparently a busy place, for it had

a good reputation and that good reputation was connected to their works. But the Lord Jesus says that He knows their works, and in His judgment, their works were imperfect. This is yet one more instance of men being impressed by something that God was not impressed with at all. God told Samuel centuries before that man looks on the outward appearance, but God looks on the heart (1 Sam. 16:7). Jesus put it even more bluntly. "And he said to them, 'You are those who justify yourselves before men, but God knows your hearts. For what is exalted among men is an abomination in the sight of God'" (Luke 16:15, ESV).

We may conclude from what is said here that the church at Sardis was virtually dead. I say virtually dead because we may put two things together. The first is that they are told they have a reputation for life, but they are, putting it simply, "dead." At the same time, the situation is not beyond hope because in the next breath they are told to strengthen the things that remain, that are *ready* to die. Putting this all together, the church corporately was dead, but there was apparently a faithful remnant there, a remnant about to die, but still capable of hearing these words of exhortation. The words that they were to obey were these—"strengthen what remains." Christians who find themselves in a similar predicament should do the same. Strengthen what you have, and don't try to do anything with what you don't have.

HOLD ON, AND REPENT

> Remember therefore how thou hast received and heard, and hold fast, and repent. If therefore thou shalt not watch, I will come on thee as a thief, and thou shalt not know what hour I will come upon thee. (Rev. 3:3)

But a handful of the saints in Sardis were still in good shape, as we will see in the next verses. They are the ones to whom this exhortation applies because they were the ones who could hear it.

The exhortation is an odd combination of "hold on" and "repent." If you had held on to this point, what is the need for repentance? If you need to repent, shouldn't the charge be to grab on? The solution to this is to remember that this is a letter to a congregation that was both dead and virtually dead. There were many who needed to grab on, and a small number who needed to hold on. In that kind of situation, where you have a basic identity shared with those who are far away from God, the charge is to repent. We might describe this as vicarious repentance. Those in Sardis who had not defiled their garments were repenting on behalf of those who had.

The prophet Daniel offered a great prayer of confession (Dan. 9:4) even though there was no evidence that he had done any of the things he was confessing. This is because we are not just distinct individuals. He was an Israelite and Israel had sinned. The saints in Sardis were in a church that had a reputation for being alive and yet was dead.

American Christians belong to a church that has grievously backslidden. How can you tell which Christians have not backslidden? They are the ones who are willing to admit that they have.

ETERNAL ELECTION

> Thou hast a few names even in Sardis which have not defiled their garments; and they shall walk with me in white: for they are worthy. He that overcometh, the same shall be clothed in white raiment; and I will not blot out his name out of the book of life, but I will confess his name before my Father, and before his angels. He that hath an ear, let him hear what the Spirit saith unto the churches. (Rev. 3:4–6)

The church at Sardis was dead and defiled both, but not each person in it. There were a few names there—and note the force of the word "few"—who had not defiled their garments. The implication is that the rest of them *had* defiled their garments. A contrast is set up between the undefiled garments now and the white garments they would be given in the future. Because they kept their garments clean in the present, they would walk with the Lord in white in the future. They are worthy, and they are overcomers.

Their names will not be blotted out of the Book of Life. If the implication is that some names will be blotted out of the Book of Life, then this means the Book of Life is the book of the covenant, and not the book of election. If the Book of Life is the book of election, then the emphasis should be on the fact that the promise is that their names would *not* be blotted out of it.

Given how the phrase is used elsewhere in Scripture, it would be best to take it as referring to decretal election. Paul rejoices in certain fellow-workers of his, "whose names are in the book of life" (Phil. 4:3). Later in Revelation, those who behold the beast in wonder are described as those whose names were not written down in the Book of Life (Rev. 17:8). And those who are truly saved, destined for Heaven, are those whose names are written then (Rev. 21:27). That which accompanies "not blotting" out names is the Lord confessing those names to His Father and to the Father's angels.

Those who have been given an ear to hear should make a point of hearing what the Spirit of God says to the churches. In Sardis, there were only a few.

STEWARD OF HISTORY

And to the angel of the church in Philadelphia write; These things saith he that is holy, he that is true, he that hath the key of David, he that openeth, and no man shutteth; and shutteth, and no man openeth. (Rev. 3:7)

The church at Philadelphia is next, and is a church that is simply praised and encouraged. They had done well, and are not admonished for any significant sin. The words to the angel of the church at Philadelphia are words from the one who is identified as "holy" and as "true." So this continues as a series of messages to the churches from the Lord Jesus.

This opening greeting to the church also contains a messianic reference from a prophecy by Isaiah. A man named Shebna had been comptroller during the reign of Hezekiah. He was a prideful man, and because of this was ejected from his place (Is. 22:15-25). He had built himself a very fancy sepulcher, which Isaiah mocked, and its lintel now occupies a place in the British Museum. Shebna was a conceited man who had removed a godly man named Eliakim from his place. Shebna was likely a traitor, or some kind of double-dealer, a man with secret communications with Judah's enemies. Ambrose Bierce calls a mausoleum the final and funniest folly of the rich, and in this case at least, God agreed. He was building a grand memory for himself in a country he was betraying, and God promised that he would be hauled off to die somewhere else.

After Shebna had received his comeuppance, Eliakim was placed in Shebna's role. There, as a faithful steward, the key of the house of David would be laid upon his shoulder. When he opened something, no one could shut it. When he shut and locked something, no one could open it. He would be permanently settled. As such, this Eliakim is a type of the Lord Jesus. Jesus is the steward of all human history, having replaced a treacherous steward, that is, the devil.

Because the key was in the possession of the Lord Jesus, the opening for the church at Philadelphia was a true opening, and would remain such.

PROGRESS BY GOD'S SPIRIT

> I know thy works: behold, I have set before thee an
> open door, and no man can shut it: for thou hast a
> little strength, and hast kept my word, and hast not
> denied my name. (Rev. 3:8)

We see in this verse a recurring biblical principle: what
belongs to Christ belongs to those who are in Christ. In the
previous verse, we saw that Christ is the one with a key
that opens what no man can shut, and who shuts what no
man can open. Because of the Lord Jesus' authority, the
words spoken in the next verse apply the very same reality
to the Christians at the church in Philadelphia.

The Lord mentions four things that relate to their faithfulness. First, He knows their works. Second, their works
were done despite having "little strength." Third, they have
kept the Lord's word, and last, they have not denied His
name. So they worked though they had little strength to
work, they kept the word that had been entrusted to them,
and they did not deny the name of the Lord. The Lord commends them for all this, but more than commending them,
He bestows on them what He only can give. He sets before
them an open door, which no man can shut.

The progress of the faithful church is never by might, or
by power, but by God's Spirit (Zech. 4:6). God is therefore
the God of disproportionate results.

FALSE JEWS

> Behold, I will make them of the synagogue of Satan, which say they are Jews, and are not, but do lie; behold, I will make them to come and worship before thy feet, and to know that I have loved thee. (Rev. 3:9)

Throughout the Old Testament a distinction is made between those Jews who knew the Lord, and those who knew the Lord in truth. This same theme is carried over into the New Testament and highlighted there, with the intent that Christians, who are members of the new Israel, would take the central lesson to heart—which is that you must be born again. Regardless of your covenant status, you must have the root of the matter within you. And the root of the matter is Christ within you, the hope of glory.

Put bluntly, if you have the covenant of God, but you do not have God Himself, then what you actually have is Satan. Nominal Christians are not partial Christians, but rather devil-worshipers. Nominal Christians are not halfway to Heaven, but rather most of the way to Hell. They are Christians in some sense, but not in any sense that is a blessing.

John here speaks fiercely of those who claimed to be Jews, but who were not. They were lying about it—whether or not they had actually descended from Abraham. They claimed they were Jewish, and they gathered in synagogues, but the whole thing was a pretense and farce.

God responds by saying that He will make them acknowledge that the Christians were the true objects of God's electing love, which would mean that they were the heirs of all

God's promises to Israel. He would make them come and prostrate themselves before them, not in worship (as though they were divine), but rather in awe and profound respect.

GETTING THE TEST OUT OF THE WAY

> Because thou hast kept the word of my patience, I also will keep thee from the hour of temptation, which shall come upon all the world, to try them that dwell upon the earth. (Rev. 3:10)

The saints in Philadelphia had remained faithful during trials up to this point, and the Lord promised to deliver them from a future trial, the kind of trial that was going to come upon the entire world. The word translated *temptation* here can be rendered either as temptation or trial, and when the Lord adds that He is going to "*try* them that dwell upon the earth," He is using the same root in a verb form. This is going to be a time of testing, a time of trial, and the church at Philadelphia wouldn't have to deal with it because they had already passed their test.

The word they kept was the word of the Lord's *patience*, which means they had gone through something that had called for patience. When they were being tried, the world was not being tried, and when the world received its great test, the church at Philadelphia was kept from it.

THE AISLE THAT COMES DOWN FROM HEAVEN

> Behold, I come quickly: hold that fast which thou hast,
> that no man take thy crown. Him that overcometh will
> I make a pillar in the temple of my God, and he shall
> go no more out: and I will write upon him the name
> of my God, and the name of the city of my God, which
> is new Jerusalem, which cometh down out of heav-
> en from my God: and I will write upon him my new
> name. He that hath an ear, let him hear what the Spirit
> saith unto the churches. (Rev. 3:11-13)

The Lord tells the believers in Philadelphia to hold on tight
to what they have, and they are to do so because the Lord
is coming "quickly." This means that the coming referred to
had relevance to them, two thousand years ago. The Lord
is encouraging them to allow no man to take their crown.
The fact that they were in present possession of that crown
meant that they were already ruling with Christ. They had a
crown they were not to surrender, and were to hold fast to it
through the coming trial that would culminate in the Lord's
coming. Comparing this passage with the rest of Revelation
we can see that this is the coming of the Lord in judgment
on Jerusalem, which was finally destroyed in 70 A.D.

The one who overcomes is going to be given rest from
battle. The expression "go no more out" is used to describe
Moses at 120 years old, unable to go across the Jordan to
the war of conquest (Dt. 31:2). And when David is almost
killed in battle and Abishai rescued him (2 Sam. 21:17),

the men of David swore that he should "go no more out." In this case, the battle would have been won, and the saints of Philadelphia are old and honored warriors, overcomers. They have been made pillars in the Temple.

The Temple is referred to again in another way. They have the name of God written on them, and they have the name of the city of God, which is the New Jerusalem, also written on them. They are pillars in that Temple and a part of the city that is built entirely out of living stones. We are being given a glimpse of the theme of the entire book of Revelation: the replacement of the old Jerusalem with the New Jerusalem, the replacement of old Israel with new Israel, and the replacement of the nation of Israel with the cosmic and ultimate city, the Church.

The Jerusalem above is the mother of us all (Gal. 4:26), the Church. The angel later in Revelation tells John that he will show him the bride, the wife of the Lamb (Rev. 21:9), and goes on to show him the New Jerusalem (Rev. 21:10). The New Jerusalem is a perfect cube, which is the shape of the Holy of Holies (1 Kings 6:20). The Christian Church is the Temple of the Holy Spirit (1 Cor. 3:16-17; 6:19), and all together we are a spiritual house (1 Pet. 2:5). The history of the world since Pentecost should be understood as *that* bride walking down *that* aisle, the great aisle that comes down from heaven.

The overcomers of Philadelphia (and every overcomer since) have three names written on them. The first is the name of God, the second is the name of the Church, and the Lord's "new name." Those who have an ear to listen should make sure they listen.

LUKEWARM WORKS

> And unto the angel of the church of the Laodiceans
> write; These things saith the Amen, the faithful and
> true witness, the beginning of the creation of God; I
> know thy works, that thou art neither cold nor hot: I
> would thou wert cold or hot. So then because thou art
> lukewarm, and neither cold nor hot, I will spue thee
> out of my mouth. (Rev. 3:14–16)

We come now to perhaps the most famous of the seven
churches of Asia. This is the lukewarm and tepid church
of the Laodiceans, the basis for many sermonic rebukes of
lethargic congregations.

The rebuke comes from the Lord, the one giving all these
messages to the angels of the respective churches. He identifies Himself here with a series of striking images. Jesus is the
ultimate Amen—Amen is one of His names. He is the faithful
and true witness (*martys*), so when we faithfully bear witness
to Him, we are bearing faithful and true witness to the faithful
and true witness. And then last, He is the *arche* of the whole
creation of God, meaning that He is the integration point of
all things. In Christ all things hold together, Paul says, going
on to use the same word (Col. 1:17-18). The Lord Jesus is the
one in whom the entire cosmos *coheres*.

The Laodiceans were lukewarm in their works. If they
had been cold, it would have been refreshing, and if they
had been hot, it would have been comforting. But as it
was, they were the room temperature church, the tepid
church. Laodicea had to pipe their water in, and Colossae

had cold springs about ten miles away. Hierapolis had hot springs, but they were about six miles away. By the time the water got to Laodicea, it was lukewarm and useless for everything except for the apostle John's metaphor.

Our works are intended as water for the Lord to drink. Cold is good, and hot is good, but tepid works are the kind that the Lord will spit out.

TRUSTING IN RICHES

> Because thou sayest, I am rich, and increased with goods, and have need of nothing; and knowest not that thou art wretched, and miserable, and poor, and blind, and naked. (Rev. 3:17)

The reason why the church at Laodicea was lukewarm was because when it came to riches, they were hot. In short, their wealth made them self-sufficient, and self-sufficiency is what lukewarmness in religion *is*. The reason the Lord would spew them out of His mouth is because they had said to themselves that they were "rich, and increased with goods." The end result of this was that they had "need of nothing," which meant they had need of nothing from the Lord. If you don't need anything, then you don't need anything from Him.

This is the perennial temptation that comes with wealth, and Scripture warns of this constantly. The Israelites were warned as they came out of the wilderness—where God gave them water from the rock and bread from the sky— that they would be tempted to this self-sufficiency. "And thou say in thine heart, My power and the might of mine hand hath gotten me this wealth" (Deut. 8:17). The rich fool looked out on his need for bigger barns with some complacency (Luke 12:18). Jesus says not to lay up treasure on earth, where moth and rust destroy (Matt. 6:19). And Paul tells the rich in this world not to trust in "uncertain riches" (1 Tim. 6:17). In short, the Laodiceans apparently thought that in their case riches would not do what riches always do.

And the apparent lack of need in one area covers over the desperate actual need in another. While they said they had "need of nothing," what did they in fact need? There is only one thing worse than being wretched, miserable, poor, blind, and naked, and that is to be all five of those things and add to it the sixth misery of not knowing about it.

GOD'S RESPONSE TO WRETCHEDNESS

> I counsel thee to buy of me gold tried in the fire, that thou mayest be rich; and white raiment, that thou mayest be clothed, and that the shame of thy nakedness do not appear; and anoint thine eyes with eyesalve, that thou mayest see. As many as I love, I rebuke and chasten: be zealous therefore, and repent. (Rev. 3:18–19)

The church at Laodicea was spiritually poor, and the likely reason was that they were *not* poor at all when it came to material goods. Laodicea was a wealthy city—it was a center for banking, and also had a thriving wool and linen industry. They were also famous for a medical school, and for an eye ointment that was made there out of Phrygian powder.

The Roman historian Tacitus wrote this about the city's recovery from a major earthquake in 60 A.D.: "Laodicea arose from the ruins by the strength of her own resources, and with no help from us" (*Annals*, xiv.27). They were rich, and the church there was an apparent partaker of the general wealth. And this meant in turn that the Christians were tempted to provide a sort of pious echo of that pagan wealth instead of offering a true alternative to it.

And so the Lord challenges them to receive true riches in place of their shadow riches—but He makes a point to use images drawn from their shadow wealth. Buy refined gold from me, gold refined in the fire (banking). Buy white raiment to cover your nakedness (textiles). Anoint your eyes with a spiritual eye salve (medicine).

There were some severe spiritual problems in the six other churches of Asia, but the Lord somehow finds something to commend with them. But not here. This church really was, from front to back, wretched, miserable, poor, blind, and naked. And yet . . .

What is the Lord's response to this wretchedness? He invites them to be zealous in repentance. And He invites them this way because, as He puts it, He loves them. Why did He rebuke and chasten them? "As many as I *love*, I rebuke and chasten."

AN INVITATION

Behold, I stand at the door, and knock: if any man hear my voice, and open the door, I will come in to him, and will sup with him, and he with me. To him that overcometh will I grant to sit with me in my throne, even as I also overcame, and am set down with my Father in

his throne. He that hath an ear, let him hear what the
Spirit saith unto the churches. (Rev. 3:20–22)

Despite the fact that the church at Laodicea was in a wretched state, the Lord still offers to commune with any who
will commune with Him. The invitation is famously stated
as though the Lord were knocking at the door of someone's
heart, but there is no mention of a heart in this text at all.
The door He is knocking on is the door of a *church*. If any
of the Laodiceans hear His voice—which indicates that He
is both knocking and calling—and comes to open the door,
the Lord promises to come in "to him" and sup with him,
and the table fellowship would be mutual. This is not a
salvation text at all—it is a reformation text.

And despite the defeated condition of that particular
church, a glorious prospect is held out. That defeated church
might have overcomers contained within it. To anyone who
overcomes, the Lord will invite him to be seated together
with Christ in His throne. This is done according to the same
logic that was applied when the Lord overcame in His trial, and was seated together with the Father in *His* throne.
As that Father shared His throne with the Son, so the Son
shares His throne with believers who overcome.

The same general invitation is given to them that is giv-
en to other churches—if a man has an ear, he should take
care to listen to what the Spirit is saying to the churches.
Here we should note the plural churches. What is said to
each church is said—*mutatis mutandis*—to them all. We
make adjustments in application in the different churches,
but there is always some application.

CHAPTER 4

SHORTLY MEANS SHORTLY

> After this I looked, and, behold, a door was opened
> in heaven: and the first voice which I heard was as it
> were of a trumpet talking with me; which said, Come
> up hither, and I will shew thee things which must be
> hereafter. (Rev. 4:1)

The first three chapters of Revelation should be considered as a preamble. John is setting the stage, describing
the reasons for the revelation that is about to be made
manifest. Remember that the entire book is going to be
read to the Philadelphians, to the Laodiceans, to the Thy-
atirans, and so on. This revelation is going to land in their

respective churches very differently. Those in Philadelphia are already overcomers, so they are ready for what this book contains. Those in Laodicea are not ready, at least not apart from repentance. The truth is always constant, but it strikes different levels of inconstancy differently.

John looked and a door in the heavens opened up. He heard a voice that was described as "the first voice," and the voice sounded like a trumpet talking. John is invited up into the heavens so that he might be shown the things which were to come "hereafter." Given what has been said in the preamble, and from details of the revelation itself, we know that these events will be *shortly* hereafter. John was not being shown the distant future. When Daniel was shown the distant future, he was told to seal the words of the prophecy because the fulfilled events were still 4 centuries in the future. John is told *not* to seal what he sees, and it would be odd if the events were 20 centuries out and counting.

The other thing to note here is that we see the development of a "two-layer" structure for the remainder of the book. Those two layers are the history of Heaven and the history of earth. God is worshiped in Heaven, and dramatic things are accomplished on earth. God is glorified in Heaven, and God is glorified on earth. And this is how we pray—may Your will be done on earth as it is in Heaven.

JESUS' THRONE

> And immediately I was in the spirit: and, behold, a throne was set in heaven, and one sat on the throne. And he that sat was to look upon like a jasper and a

sardine stone: and there was a rainbow round about
the throne, in sight like unto an emerald. (Rev. 4:2–3)

When the heavens open and John is invited up, he says that he was immediately "in the spirit" (v. 2). This is the second time this has happened in the book—the first is when he received the initial vision of the Lord Jesus walking among the churches (Rev. 1:10). Here is the vision of the Lord Jesus enthroned in Heaven.

This vision is very similar to the vision that Ezekiel saw at the beginning of his book (Ezek. 1:26-28). Here it says that the color of the one who sat on the throne was like jasper, which can be red, yellow, brown or green. Sardius (known to us as carnelian) is red in color. In Ezekiel, the one who sat on the throne was described as the color of amber in the midst of fire. Here in Revelation, there is a rainbow around the throne, but the rainbow is described as emerald green. In Ezekiel, it is simply described as a rainbow. Clearly John is functioning in an intertextual way, wanting us to think of Ezekiel's vision while at the same time developing it. The bow is *around* the throne, and so we should think of it as having a halo effect.

The first color mentioned is the color of jasper, which was the *last* stone in the high priest's breastplate (Ex. 28:20; Ex. 39:13). The second stone mentioned here is sardius, which is the first stone in that same breastplate (Ex. 28:17).

RULING ELDERS

And round about the throne were four and twenty
seats: and upon the seats I saw four and twenty elders

> sitting, clothed in white raiment; and they had on their
> heads crowns of gold. (Rev. 4:4)

And so we come to the part of this book where it is necessary to start "identifying" things. You cannot interpret without interpreting, and so here we go.

I take the twenty-four elders to be representative of the elect of God throughout all history. There were twelve tribes in the Old Testament and twelve apostles in the New, giving us twenty-four. The number twenty-four is also evocative of the priesthood, which in the time of David was divided into twenty-four courses (1 Chron. 24:4; 25:9-13). In his vision, Ezekiel saw twenty-five men—the high priest along with the heads of the twenty-four orders of priests (Ezek. 8:16; 11:1). We have the same thing here. The High Priest is on His throne, and around Him are the twenty-four elders. These men show that God through the salvation wrought by Christ is reconstituting the earthly component of His Divine Council, as drawn from among men.

These men are called elders (*presbyteros*), and they also have crowns, which makes them ruling elders. They also have other indications of their priestly function as they are dressed in white, and they offer incense (Rev. 5:8).

These functions together (kings and priests) fit with the self-description of the elders in the next chapter (Rev. 5:10). The elders clearly represent elect mankind because they confess that the Lamb redeemed them with His blood, and has made them "kings and priests." Their rule is on the earth, and that rule is about to be manifested through the course of the rest of the book.

JESUS' LAMPSTAND

> And out of the throne proceeded lightnings and thun-
> derings and voices: and there were seven lamps of fire
> burning before the throne, which are the seven Spirits
> of God. (Rev. 4:5)

Around the throne were twenty-four seats for the elders. *From* the throne were thunder and lightning and voices, and *before* the throne were seven fiery lamps.

The awe-inspiring spectacle of what was proceeding from the throne—voices, thunder, lightning—conjure up images of Sinai. Just as God manifested Himself in terrifying ways with the first covenant, so also with the second. The author of Hebrews concurs with this, saying that Sinai, a mountain that could be touched in principle was still prohibited to the touch (Heb. 12:18ff). Sinai was characterized by fire, blackness, darkness, and these *voices*. It was terrifying, but the mountain of the new covenant is even more so (Heb. 10:28-29).

Commentators are divided on the seven lamps. The majority view is that this is a numerical representation of the Holy Spirit, with seven as the number of perfection. This has strong support from the fact that the text identifies them *as* "the seven Spirits of God." But remember that the Lord Jesus, the one who sits on the throne, walks in the midst of seven lampstands, and these lampstands are the seven churches addressed by this book (Rev. 1:12). The words used for candlestick and lampstand are different words, but this does not make identification impossible.

Also suggestive is the idea that the lampstand in front of the throne here is the celestial menorah. Remember that the original menorah, the one used in the Temple, had seven lights.

FOUR LIVING CREATURES

> And before the throne there was a sea of glass like unto crystal: and in the midst of the throne, and round about the throne, were four beasts full of eyes before and behind. And the first beast was like a lion, and the second beast like a calf, and the third beast had a face as a man, and the fourth beast was like a flying eagle. (Rev. 4:6–7)

There are two realities to be interpreted here. The first is the crystal sea. The word is *thalassa*, which is the word for lake or sea, but it is referring to the heavenly version of the artificial sea that God had Solomon establish in the temple (2 Chron. 4:2-6). In the earthly temple, this is where the priests would purify themselves. Our great high priest has no need of purification, and the bronze sea is now a crystal sea.

It was common for ancient kings to have their thrones settled upon statues of creatures, as Solomon's throne was established on lions. But those were carved creatures, and these are *living* creatures. The four living creatures most likely answer to the cherubim in Ezekiel's vision, with this difference. Each of the four cherubim in Ezekiel have four faces. The same four faces appear here, but each of the cherubim has just one.

These living creatures are in the midst of the throne, and also are around it. The rabbis interpreted the faces to mean king of the wild beasts (lion), king of the domestic beasts (ox), the king of all birds (eagle), and the king of all creatures (man). There appears to be some connection between the cherubim and man in Christ because in v. 9 we see that whenever they give glory to the one who sits on the throne, the twenty-four elders follow suit and fall down before Him.

A COUPLE OF PRAYING JALAPEÑOS

> And the four beasts had each of them six wings about him; and they were full of eyes within: and they rest not day and night, saying, Holy, holy, holy, Lord God Almighty, which was, and is, and is to come. (Rev. 4:8)

The four beasts here are cherubim, as we find them in Ezekiel, but they have certain things in common with the seraphim found in Isaiah 6. For example, both cherubim and seraphim have six wings, and both of them are overflowing with adoration, crying out *holy, holy, holy*. The cherubim praise the Lord God Almighty, the one who was, is, and who is to come. The seraphim go on to extol the Lord of hosts, and say that the whole earth is full of His glory. But in both cases, we find angelic beings with six wings who sing praise to the thrice-named holiness of God.

These are "full of eyes," as were Ezekiel's cherubim (Ezek. 1:18), and they are creatures who do not need to take any rest, day or night. Being so close to the one who neither slumbers nor sleeps, they imitate Him in the same.

This is as good a place as any to note that cherubim are not chubby Renaissance babies with six-inch wings. It is six wings, not six-inch wings. And neither are they the angelic human figures of popular Christian art, with huge white feathery wings coming out their shoulder blades. Think of something more like the sphinx, or a great winged Assyrian bull with a man's head and a full square beard. In other words, you have likely never seen—whether in a Picture Bible or in a more scholarly study Bible—*any* picture of the Ark of the Covenant that represents even remotely what it actually looked like.

One time I saw a replica of the Ark that had two kneeling human figures that were completely covered with their wings, so that they looked for all the world like a couple of praying jalapeños. But we should not tarry with these matters. We should move on to the next verse.

SIMPLY BECAUSE HE WANTED TO

> And when those beasts give glory and honour and thanks to him that sat on the throne, who liveth for ever and ever, The four and twenty elders fall down before him that sat on the throne, and worship him that liveth for ever and ever, and cast their crowns before the throne, saying, Thou art worthy, O Lord, to receive glory and honour and power: for thou hast created all things, and for thy pleasure they are and were created. (Rev. 4:9–11)

The four beasts are cherubim, surrounding the throne of the one who lives forever and ever. In the Old Testament, there were two cherubim surrounding the mercy seat on the Ark of the Covenant. Here the cherubim are alive, not gold (Ex. 25:18)—they are *living* creatures, and there are four of them, not two. But they still surround the mercy seat—the throne of the Lamb is the ultimate seat of mercy.

The cherubim set the pitch for worship. It says that when they give glory, honor and thanks to Christ, the twenty-four elders follow suit. We have already touched on the fact that the twenty-four elders represent the elect of God throughout all history, twelve tribes in the Old Testament and twelve apostles in the New. All the redeemed throughout all history give honor and praise. The cherubim are the pitch pipe, and when they have rendered their glory, the twenty-four elders do the same thing. They all fall down before the one who sits on the throne, and who lives forever and ever. As they fall prostrate, they cast their crowns in front of the throne. The fact that they *have* crowns means that they are kings themselves, and that their seats are in fact lesser thrones. In fact, where the AV translates it as *seats*, the Greek word there is *thronos*. The Lord Jesus is in fact the King of kings.

The cherubim give glory, honor and thanks. The elders declare that the Lord is worthy of such praise, and they modify the declaration slightly. They say that He is worthy to receive glory, honor, and *power*. They say that He is worthy of such worship because He is the one who created absolutely everything, and they go on to tell us why the Lord created them all. The AV says that He created them for His pleasure. The word is *will*, and it would be better to say that He created all things for the sake of His good pleasure—in other words, simply because He wanted to.

CHAPTER 5

TWO WAYS

> And I saw in the right hand of him that sat on the
> throne a book written within and on the backside,
> sealed with seven seals. And I saw a strong angel pro-
> claiming with a loud voice, Who is worthy to open the
> book, and to loose the seals thereof? And no man in
> heaven, nor in earth, neither under the earth, was able
> to open the book, neither to look thereon. And I wept
> much, because no man was found worthy to open and
> to read the book, neither to look thereon. (Rev. 5:1–4)

Let us first simply state what these verses *say*. We may
then step back for a better view of what they mean. The

one who sits on the throne is God Himself, because in v. 7 the Lamb comes and takes the book from Him. So then we have a book that is given by the Father to the Son. The book was held in the Father's right hand, and the Son is enthroned on the Father's right hand. The writing in the book was on both sides of the parchment, it was covered with writing both front and back. The scroll was rolled up and was sealed with seven seals. Absolutely no one in Heaven, on earth, or under the earth was able to unseal the book or able even to look at it. And so John wept because there was no one worthy to open the book, read the book, or look at the book.

So what is the *meaning* of the book? The book is *The Book of the Reign of Jesus Christ*. We know this from what is said when the Lamb is given the book, and we know it from what happens when the seals of the book are opened in the next chapter. When the Lamb takes the book, the four cherubim and the twenty-four elders all fell down and worshiped Him. They say that He is worthy to unseal the book because He had been slain, and had redeemed a people for Himself out of every tribe and nation. He had done this so that they would be made *kings and priests*, in order to *reign on the earth*.

This reign of Jesus is both welcomed and opposed. Those who welcome it worship Him. Those who oppose it are destroyed by Him. So the reign of Jesus Christ has ramifications. Those ramifications are, respectively, worship and destruction. The book is given to the Lamb in chapter five, where He is worshiped by those who see what is coming.

The book is unsealed in chapter six, and all who oppose Him are taken out, one by one.

THE LAMB AND HIS HORNS AND EYES

> And one of the elders saith unto me, Weep not: behold, the Lion of the tribe of Juda, the Root of David, hath prevailed to open the book, and to loose the seven seals thereof. And I beheld, and, lo, in the midst of the throne and of the four beasts, and in the midst of the elders, stood a Lamb as it had been slain, having seven horns and seven eyes, which are the seven Spirits of God sent forth into all the earth. (Rev. 5:5–6)

John had been lamenting that no one was available to open the scroll with seven seals. Indeed, no one was even worthy to look at it.

But one of the twenty-four elders spoke to him to encourage him. Do not weep, he said, but rather *behold*. John hears these words first, and the words tell him then to look. The real surprise does not come until he looks and sees. John is told that someone from the tribe of Judah had "prevailed." In other words, this one had overcome, He had conquered, and as a result of this conquest he was able to open the book, and to release the seven seals.

We move with John from words to sight. And what John is commanded to *behold* is a Lion. And he looks, and he *beheld* a Lamb. This Lion is from the tribe of Judah. We know from elsewhere that the Lord was descended from David, but here it says rather that David was descended from Him. He is the *Root* of David, David grew from Him. The Lord

Himself made a similar point when He asked how David's son could at the same time be David's Lord (Mark 12:37).

From the heavenly vantage point, from what the twenty-four elders knew, this great one was the Lion. But when John looks, he sees a Lamb. But there are mysteries surrounding even this. The Lamb is standing in the midst of the throne, the place of God. The Lamb had been *slain*, and yet He was *standing*.

The Lamb is clearly divine. He has seven horns, which represent the perfection of omnipotence. He has seven eyes, which represent the perfection of omniscience. These seven eyes are also identified with the seven spirits of God, which are sent out throughout the entire earth. Given that these spirits are described as the seven spirits of God, both here and earlier (Rev. 4:5), and given that they are identified with the omniscience of the slain but standing Lamb, the conclusion seems necessary that this is the Holy Spirit.

VISIBLE REIGNS

> And he came and took the book out of the right hand of him that sat upon the throne. And when he had taken the book, the four beasts and four and twenty elders fell down before the Lamb, having every one of them harps, and golden vials full of odours, which are the prayers of saints. And they sung a new song, saying, Thou art worthy to take the book, and to open the seals thereof: for thou wast slain, and hast redeemed us to God by thy blood out of every kindred, and tongue, and people, and nation; And hast made us

unto our God kings and priests: and we shall reign on
the earth. (Rev. 5:7–10)

The Lamb who was the Lion then came and took the scroll
out of the right hand of the one who sat upon the throne.
And when He had done so, the heavenly authorities and the
representatives of the entire historic church fell down before Him. All of them had harps, and bowls full of incense.
The incense is defined here as symbolic of the prayers of
the saints. This is additional confirmation on the identity
of the twenty-four elders—the prayers of the saints are, in
effect, offered by them. And secondly, this tells us how God
receives the prayers of the saints. It tells us what He thinks
about our prayers—they are a sweet-smelling odor to Him.
It is possible that the particular prayers of the saints that
are in view here are the prayers of the saints who are un-
dergoing persecution (Rev. 6:10), those who are praying
for deliverance.

The earlier song that was sung (4:11) was a song that emphasized *creation*. When this song is offered, it is described
as a *new* song, and the theme of it is *redemption*. The Lamb
is worthy to take the scroll and to open the seven seals of
that scroll because He was slain, and His blood was used to
redeem His people. The elders here say "us," meaning that
they were included in that redemption. Not only were they
redeemed, but they were redeemed out of every group of
people on earth: all kindreds and tongues, all peoples and
nations. Not only were they taken out of all these groups
all over the earth, but they have now been established as
kings and priests "on the earth." This means that their reign

is not invisible and spiritual in the heavens, and it is not an invisible reign over their own spirits. We are talking about the rise and ascendancy of the Christian faith.

There are three places in the book of Revelation where believers are described as kings and priests: Rev. 1:6, here in Rev. 5:10, and again in Rev. 20:6. It is a recurring theme. If we are kings and priests on the earth, then beware of those who teach that we are no such thing.

ALL CREATION SINGS

> And I beheld, and I heard the voice of many angels round about the throne and the beasts and the elders: and the number of them was ten thousand times ten thousand, and thousands of thousands; Saying with a loud voice, Worthy is the Lamb that was slain to receive power, and riches, and wisdom, and strength, and honour, and glory, and blessing. And every creature which is in heaven, and on the earth, and under the earth, and such as are in the sea, and all that are in them, heard I saying, Blessing, and honour, and glory, and power, be unto him that sitteth upon the throne, and unto the Lamb for ever and ever. And the four beasts said, Amen. And the four and twenty elders fell down and worshipped him that liveth for ever and ever. (Rev. 5:11–14)

We are building to a great crescendo of praise and adoration. If the Lamb were not God Himself, if Christ were not divine, then the honors rendered to Him here would indeed be blasphemous idolatry.

In this portion of Revelation, we have seen different songs of praise. The 24 elders sang first to God, to the one who sits on the throne (Rev. 4:11). The next song is rendered to the Lamb (Rev. 5:9-10), and joined by the cherubim. In this iteration of their song, they are joined by innumerable angels (Rev. 5:12), a choir that has to number in the millions. The words used are *myriad* and *chiliad*, meaning ten thousand and thousand respectively. We thus have ten thousands of ten thousands and thousands of thousands, and John says they were all singing with a *loud* voice. I dare say it was loud. After they had praised the worth of the Lamb, the whole created order—in heaven, on earth, and under the earth—all joined in with their praise of the one who sits on the throne and to the Lamb (Rev. 5:13).

The angels declare that the Lamb, having been slain, is worthy of what He has received: power, wealth, wisdom, might, honor, glory, and blessing. The entire created order says something similar—to God and to the Lamb be blessing, honor, glory, and might, forever and ever.

In response to this great chorus, the cherubim, the living creatures, say amen, and the elders fall down and worship.

CHAPTER 6

THE HORSEMAN OF CHRIST

> And I saw when the Lamb opened one of the seals, and
> I heard, as it were the noise of thunder, one of the four
> beasts saying, Come and see. And I saw, and behold a
> white horse: and he that sat on him had a bow; and
> a crown was given unto him: and he went forth con-
> quering, and to conquer. (Rev. 6:1–2)

We now come to one of the most famous set pieces out of
the book of Revelation, which is the introduction of the
four horsemen of the Apocalypse. And we also come to the
point where Christian interpreters shake hands with each

other in order to part company, not to be reunited again until the resurrection of the dead in chapter twenty.

For example, this first horseman, the one going forth conquering and to conquer, is variously interpreted. Some take him as Christ. Others taken him as Antichrist. Some take him as a series of Roman emperors. Others take him as one Roman emperor, which is to say, Vespasian. When it comes to these varied interpretations, it is not really possible to split the difference. The only true way is to interpret it with a clean conscience before God, and a spirit of charity toward those who differ.

This first aspect of this vision is declared by one of the four living beasts, who says *come and see* in a voice like thunder. If you take the rider of the white horse to be Christ, as I do, you still have a subsequent decision to make. Some take it as Christ in the form of the preached gospel, Christ in His capacity as *savior*. Others, among whom I would number myself, see the loosing of the seals as the run-up to the destruction of Jerusalem in 70 A.D. The Lord was the one who leveled that city, and so it is not out of line for us to see the Lord Christ here in His capacity as *judge*. He brings war upon the city that rejected Him, and following after Him are the other horsemen that invariably accompany conquest and war.

If the content of the scroll is the reign and rule of Jesus Christ, as we saw earlier, it is fitting that we see Him having a bow and being given a crown with the loosing of the first seal. It is fitting that He goes forth conquering and to conquer. But remember that the scroll is not opened until *all* the seals are loosed. We are being introduced to the players with the loosing of each seal. The action does not start until the scroll is finally opened.

THE HORSEMAN OF WAR

> And when he had opened the second seal, I heard the second beast say, Come and see. And there went out another horse that was red: and power was given to him that sat thereon to take peace from the earth, and that they should kill one another: and there was given unto him a great sword. (Rev. 6:3–4)

The second seal is opened, and a rider on a red horse goes out. The first seal released a rider representing victory or conquest, which I take to be the Lord Jesus. The second seal releases a horse that is the color of bloodshed, the color of a god of war. Once again John is invited to "come and see," which he does.

The thing to keep in mind is that the book of Revelation is about the replacement of the old Jerusalem below with the new Jerusalem coming down out of Heaven like a bride. In order to make way for the new Jerusalem, the old Jerusalem must be destroyed, just as Jesus had predicted. Indicating the Temple, He said that not one stone was going to be left on top of another (Mark 13:2). So in the first instance, what this means is that we should look for the fulfillment of all these troubles in the cataclysm that came upon the land of *Israel*.

This passage says that peace was going to be taken from the *ge*. A better translation than *earth* for this word would be *land*. The tribulation was coming down upon the land. Jesus predicted that it would be like no other tribulation ever, and as the history books show, that is exactly what happened to the land of Israel between the years 66 and 70 A.D.

The fighting in that war began in Galilee, and not only between Romans and Jews, but also among rival factions of the Jews. The bloodshed was terrible. By the time they were forced back to the defense of Jerusalem, there were three or four rival camps among the Jews.

The Lord Jesus said that they did not know what would make for their peace (Luke 19:42). They certainly did not. And in the next breath, the Lord spoke of the Romans leveling the city (Luke 19:43-44). The rider on the red horse rode into Israel, and he took their peace entirely away. It was not for nothing he was given a sword.

THE HORSEMAN OF FAMINE

> And when he had opened the third seal, I heard the third beast say, Come and see. And I beheld, and lo a black horse; and he that sat on him had a pair of balances in his hand. And I heard a voice in the midst of the four beasts say, A measure of wheat for a penny, and three measures of barley for a penny; and see thou hurt not the oil and the wine. (Rev. 6:5–6)

Now we come to the third seal, and the third horseman of the Apocalypse. Just as with the first two, one of the living beasts invites John to "come and see." John does so, and he sees the destructiveness of famine. We can tell that this is the horseman representing famine by what he carries (balances), and by what the voice from the midst of the four beasts says. The pronouncement is about the cost of food, about which more in a minute. In addition, we have some background information from the Old Testament.

"And when I have broken the staff of your bread, ten women shall bake your bread in one oven, and they shall deliver you your bread again by weight: and ye shall eat, and not be satisfied" (Lev. 26:26).

In other words, eating your bread by weight or by measure is an indication of a shortage of bread, and this horseman rides out with a pair of balances in hand. We also have the association of the color black with famine: "Our skin was black like an oven because of the terrible famine" (Lam. 5:10).

During the siege of Jerusalem (which is what this prophecy is about), there was a terrible famine. Though much food had been stored in Jerusalem, the rival factions among the rebels would periodically destroy the supplies of the other factions. The end result was, naturally, a terrible famine. That black horse did ride through Jerusalem.

Note the echoes of this language in what Josephus wrote about the siege.

"Many there were indeed who sold what they had for one quart; it was of wheat, if they were of the richer sort, but of barley if they were poorer" (Wars 5.10.2).

A denarius was the average pay for the average worker of that time, rendered here by the AV as "penny." And a measure of wheat is what it would take to feed that man for a day. If he wanted to feed a family, he would have to resort to barley. The grain was affected, but not the oil and wine.

THE HORSEMAN OF DEATH

> And when he had opened the fourth seal, I heard the
> voice of the fourth beast say, Come and see. And I
> looked, and behold a pale horse: and his name that sat
> on him was Death, and Hell followed with him. And
> power was given unto them over the fourth part of the
> earth, to kill with sword, and with hunger, and with
> death, and with the beasts of the earth. (Rev. 6:7–8)

The fourth seal is now opened, and as before, the next
living beast cries out to come and see. John looked, and
he saw a sickly green horse ride out. The word translated
pale here is *chloros,* which means we shouldn't lose the
greenish tint to this pestilence. Death rides the horse, and
Hades follows after. (*Hades* is the Greek word translated
as Hell by the King James Version.) It is important for us
to distinguish Hades from Hell. The former is the place
of the dead, a place of shades. In the Old Testament it is
called Sheol. Hell is the final judgment, the lake of fire,
into which Death and Hades will eventually be cast. Hades and Hell are different because Hades itself is finally
thrown into Hell, the lake of fire (Rev. 20:14).

So Death rides the horse, slaying a fourth part of those
before him, and Hades follows after, like a wagon meant
to gather up the bodies. Death kills by four means—by the
sword, by famine, by pestilence, and by wild animals. This
passage contains an echo of Ezekiel 14:21, which refers to
the destruction of Jerusalem by the Babylonians.

"For thus saith the Lord God; How much more when I send my four sore judgments upon Jerusalem, the sword, and the famine, and the noisome beast, and the pestilence, to cut off from it man and beast?" (Ezek. 14:21).

The Romans were to bring upon Jerusalem exactly the same kind of judgment that Babylon had brought. They marched on it with the sword, besieged it with their army, shut them up to famine and pestilence within, and there were more than enough dead bodies for the ravaging dogs.

WAITING FOR ALL THE MARTYRS

And when he had opened the fifth seal, I saw under the altar the souls of them that were slain for the word of God, and for the testimony which they held: And they cried with a loud voice, saying, How long, O Lord, holy and true, dost thou not judge and avenge our blood on them that dwell on the earth? And white robes were given unto every one of them; and it was said unto them, that they should rest yet for a little season, until their fellowservants also and their brethren, that should be killed as they were, should be fulfilled. (Rev. 6:9–11)

There are only four horsemen and there are seven seals. This means that the last three seals represent the affliction that is coming down on Jerusalem in a different way.

The Old Testament teaches us that the blood of the sacrificial victims was poured out at the foot of the altar. "And the priest . . . shall pour all the blood of the bullock at the bottom of the altar of the burnt offering" (Lev. 4:7). This is what was done with the burnt offering, which was an ascension offering, an offering of entire consecration. We are also taught in Leviticus that the soul (*nephesh*) of the flesh is in the blood. "For the life of the flesh is in the blood: and I have given it to you upon the altar to make an atonement for your souls: for it is the blood that maketh an atonement for the soul" (Lev. 17:11). So when we find the souls of the martyrs under the altar in Heaven, we are meant to think of this sacrificial imagery. This does not compete with the once-for-all sacrifice of Christ on the cross, but there is some sense in which the martyrs fill up the sufferings of Christ (Col. 1:24). This is because we are the body of Christ. When Saul was tormenting the saints on earth, the Lord Jesus asked him this from Heaven: "Why do you persecute *me*?" (Acts 22:7).

The martyrs were slain for two reasons. The first was the Word of God, and the second was their own testimony (*marturia*). From this exalted position under the altar of God, they cry out for judgment and vengeance. As true saints have always done, they leave this vindication in the hands of God, while urging Him to delay no longer than necessary. They are told to be patient and to wait until the full number of martyrs has come in. We can see they are righteous from the white robes they are given.

There are a number of indications that the persecution referred to here is the persecution of the first generation of Christians by the Jews. The martyrs cry out for vengeance against those who dwell upon the earth, which could be rendered as *land*.

In addition, Jerusalem had a reputation for dealing violently with prophets. "Nevertheless I must walk to day, and to morrow, and the day following: for it cannot be that a prophet perish out of Jerusalem" (Luke 13:33). The divine blow for this blood guilt was going to land upon Jerusalem, and upon the generation that had slain Jesus. "That upon you may come all the righteous blood shed upon the earth, from the blood of righteous Abel unto the blood of Zacharias son of Barachias, whom ye slew between the temple and the altar" (Matt. 23:35). "Then answered all the people, and said, His blood be on us, and on our children" (Matt. 27:25). There is no reason to suppose that the cry for vengeance under the altar is changing the subject. And when Jesus told the parable of the unjust judge, He wrapped it up with language that sounds very much like the voices from underneath the altar. "And shall not God avenge his own elect, which cry day and night unto him, though he bear long with them? I tell you that he will avenge them speedily. Nevertheless when the Son of man cometh, shall he find faith on the earth?" (Luke 18:7–8).

How long would the souls under the altar have to wait? Until the full number of martyrs had come in, and then God's vengeance would fall upon Jerusalem. That happened in 70 A.D.

TOTAL JUDGMENT

> And I beheld when he had opened the sixth seal, and, lo, there was a great earthquake; and the sun became black as sackcloth of hair, and the moon became as

blood; And the stars of heaven fell unto the earth, even as a fig tree casteth her untimely figs, when she is shaken of a mighty wind. And the heaven departed as a scroll when it is rolled together; and every mountain and island were moved out of their places. And the kings of the earth, and the great men, and the rich men, and the chief captains, and the mighty men, and every bondman, and every free man, hid themselves in the dens and in the rocks of the mountains; And said to the mountains and rocks, Fall on us, and hide us from the face of him that sitteth on the throne, and from the wrath of the Lamb: For the great day of his wrath is come; and who shall be able to stand? (Rev. 6:12-17)

When the sixth seal is opened, we are dealing with a dark apocalypse. It would be easy to place these events at the end of the world—since only the end of the world, we think, would have enough room for a disaster this size. But we tend to think this way because we do not let the Scriptures instruct us *how* disaster symbolism works.

First there is a great earthquake, which in Scripture is a regular way to indicate a divine visitation. For this, see Ex. 19:18, Is. 2:19, or Hag. 2:6. The language that follows is "decreation" language, language of destruction. This collapsing solar system imagery is common in Scripture, and always refers to the annihilation of a nation or city/state. Isaiah speaks this way of Babylon (Is. 13:1-10). Later Isaiah speaks of the destruction of Edom in the same way (Is. 34:4). Ezekiel speaks of Egypt's fall with these terms (Ezek.

32:7-8). Joel prophesies the end of Israel in the first century with this language (Joel 2:28-32). Amos does the same thing concerning the northern kingdom of Israel (Amos 8:9). And to top it off, the Lord Jesus quotes the passages from Isaiah in order to answer the questions about what was going to happen to Jerusalem (Matt. 24:29, 34).

In addition, John here uses Isaiah's picture of stars falling like figs and of the heavens being rolled up like a scroll (Is. 34:4). And Christ Himself predicted that refugees from the fighting in Jerusalem would in fact seek refuge in caves and under rocks (Luke 23:28-31), and He was drawing on Hos. 10:8, Is. 2:10, 19, and 21 when He did this. Incidentally, Josephus tells us that this is exactly what happened (*Wars* 6.7.3).

The earthquake represents a revolution in government, an overthrow. The sun, moon, and stars represent the various dignitaries of the governmental firmament. Seven aspects of the created order are mentioned—earth, sun, moon, stars, sky, mountains, and islands. In addition, seven different kinds of men are mentioned—kings, great men, rich men, chief captains, mighty men, slaves, and free men. In short, the revolution accomplished here is total and encompasses everyone.

This context helps to answer the objection that his kind of "cosmic destruction" language is kind of overdone if we are merely talking about the destruction of just one city. There are two answers to this. One is that the destruction of Jerusalem in 70 A.D. was horrific on its own terms, even if we were simply talking about it as a stand-alone event. "For then shall be great tribulation, such as was not since the beginning of the world to this time, no, nor ever shall be" (Matt. 24:21). But the second thing to note is that Jerusalem is where God had set His name to dwell. These were the chosen people, this was the chosen city, this mountain was the chosen mountain. And in response to the prayer of the apostles, *this* mountain was plucked up and thrown into the sea (Matt. 21:21). It was the close of an *aeon*, and the world was utterly transformed. This transformation was so total, so complete, and so massive, we can't even see it.

CHAPTER 7

JESUS ON OUR FOREHEAD

And after these things I saw four angels standing on the four corners of the earth, holding the four winds of the earth, that the wind should not blow on the earth, nor on the sea, nor on any tree. And I saw another angel ascending from the east, having the seal of the living God: and he cried with a loud voice to the four angels, to whom it was given to hurt the earth and the sea, Saying, Hurt not the earth, neither the sea, nor the trees, till we have sealed the servants of our God in their foreheads. (Rev. 7:1–3)

Six seals have been opened, and before the seventh is broken, the apostle John gives us a reprise of the first four seals. You recall that the first four seals were the destructive forces of the four horsemen of the Apocalypse. Here we have four angels at the four corners of the earth, holding back the destructive "four winds" of the earth. We can make this connection because in the parallel passage in Zechariah 6:3-5, we have the four horsemen also, but they are identified with spirits or winds. "And the angel answered and said unto me, These are the four spirits [winds] of the heavens, which go forth from standing before the Lord of all the earth" (Zech. 6:5). Remember that God makes His angels winds, His servants flames of fire (Ps. 104:4; Heb. 1:7).

As John has been describing the destruction that is going to be visited upon Jerusalem, the natural question arises. Will God's people be spared? Yes. The Lord told His disciples to flee when they saw Jerusalem surrounded by armies (Luke 21:20-21), which they did, taking refuge in Pella. This protection is signified by means of an angel marking God's elect on the forehead. What God did in the destruction of Jerusalem in 70 A.D. had an earlier parallel when that same city was destroyed by the Babylonians in 586 B.C. Before that earlier judgment God sent an angel to mark His own on *their* foreheads (Ezek. 9).

The forehead is significant. *Holiness to the Lord* was bound to Aaron's forehead (Ex. 28:36-38). In a way directly contrary, the name of the great Harlot was bound to her forehead (Rev. 17:5). The mark of the beast, without which no one could buy or sell, was a mark on the right hand or on the forehead (Rev. 13:17). This was a gross parody of what God required of His people, which was to bind His law on their right hands or on their foreheads (Dt. 6:8). Our allegiance to Jesus Christ should be as obvious to the world as our forehead is.

The previous chapter of Revelation had concluded with the pressing question—who is able to stand in the day of God's great wrath? In a time like this, that is *the* question. John has Malachi 3:2 in mind, and the answer to that question is the seal of God. So four angels were holding back the four winds of the previously described destruction on the land, and those angels were told to restrain the judgment until a fifth angel, ascending out the east like a rising sun, with a seal in his hand, would be able to apply that seal to God's own children. They were told not to hurt the earth, the sea, or the trees, until the seal of God had been applied to the sons and daughters of God. God never sends His judgments in before He sends the sealing angel in.

OPENING THE SCROLL

And I heard the number of them which were sealed: and there were sealed an hundred and forty and four thousand of all the tribes of the children of Israel. Of the tribe of Juda were sealed twelve thousand. Of the tribe of Reuben were sealed twelve thousand. Of the tribe of Gad were sealed twelve thousand. Of the tribe of Aser were sealed twelve thousand. Of the tribe of Nepthalim were sealed twelve thousand. Of the tribe of Manasses were sealed twelve thousand. Of the tribe

of Simeon were sealed twelve thousand. Of the tribe
of Levi were sealed twelve thousand. Of the tribe of
Issachar were sealed twelve thousand. Of the tribe of
Zabulon were sealed twelve thousand. Of the tribe of
Joseph were sealed twelve thousand. Of the tribe of
Benjamin were sealed twelve thousand. (Rev. 7:4–8)

So now we come to the 144,000. Before getting to what
that number represents, we should first consider how it
was derived. A basic military unit in ancient Israel was a
chiliad, a thousand men (Num. 31:4-5). If you take the
number of tribes, which is 12, and square that number,
you get 144. Multiply by a thousand, and you have a symbolic number for the host of Israel.

Another thing we should take note of is the fact that the
tribes are listed out of their usual order. The tribe of Judah comes first, the tribe of the Christ. The tribe of Dan is
missing, and Joseph is listed as a tribe instead of Ephraim.
Some have assumed that Dan and Ephraim, tribes that had
a special problem with idolatry, are missing for that reason.

Among those who believe the book of Revelation was
largely fulfilled in the first century, the common assumption
is that the 144,000 is a number that symbolizes the full and
complete number of Jewish Christians who escaped death
when the city of Jerusalem was demolished in 70 A.D. This
has the advantage of keeping the interpretation anchored
in the first century, where the action of this book largely is.

But at the same time, there is an indication of a much
more cosmic interpretation, which is that the number represents the entire number of the elect. The argument for this

is that John *heard* the number 144,000, while in the next verse, John turned and looked and *saw* a multitude that no one could number. This appears to be the elect, and it also appears to be a visual representation of the symbolic number he had just heard. This is the approach I would favor.

Some think that it is odd that the Christian church would be listed by tribe, but it is symbolically fitting. There is a reason why Christ selected 12 apostles. The church is identified with the true Israel elsewhere (Gal. 6:16; Eph. 2:12).

CHURCH MILITANT, CHURCH TRIUMPHANT

After this I beheld, and, lo, a great multitude, which no man could number, of all nations, and kindreds, and people, and tongues, stood before the throne, and before the Lamb, clothed with white robes, and palms in their hands; And cried with a loud voice, saying, Salvation to our God which sitteth upon the throne, and unto the Lamb. And all the angels stood round about the throne, and about the elders and the four beasts, and fell before the throne on their faces, and worshipped God, Saying, Amen: Blessing, and glory, and wisdom, and thanksgiving, and honour, and power, and might, be unto our God for ever and ever. Amen. And one of the elders answered, saying unto me, What are these which are arrayed in white robes? and whence came they? And I said unto him, Sir, thou knowest. And he said to me, These are they which came out of great tribulation, and have washed their robes, and made them white in the blood of the Lamb.

Therefore are they before the throne of God, and serve him day and night in his temple: and he that sitteth on the throne shall dwell among them. They shall hunger no more, neither thirst any more; neither shall the sun light on them, nor any heat. For the Lamb which is in the midst of the throne shall feed them, and shall lead them unto living fountains of waters: and God shall wipe away all tears from their eyes. (Rev. 7:9–17)

Having heard the number of 144,000, John turns, looks and sees this innumerable host. The earlier number is specifically cited as being numbered as Israel, and this throng is from all nations, peoples, languages, etc. Some believe this necessitates taking them as distinct groups. I follow the other view which takes the symbolic number of Israel as representing the innumerable host of the Church. The previous group was *sealed* on earth and the latter group is *saved* in Heaven.

So this great multitude is dressed in white, symbolizing purity, and they are holding palm branches, which symbolizes victory. Dressed this way, and holding their palms, they stood before the throne and the Lamb, and they cried out. How loud might an innumerable host be? They cried out in order to ascribe salvation to God, the God who was seated on the throne, as well as to the Lamb. At that point, the angels, the twenty-four elders, and the four living creatures all prostrated themselves in order to worship God. And they said, "Amen: Blessing, and glory, and wisdom, and thanksgiving, and honor, and power, and might, be unto our God for ever and ever. Amen."

One of the twenty-four elders asked John if he knew the identity of the great crowd. He confessed that he did not. The elder says that they are the ones who came out of the great tribulation. If this crowd is identified with the church through the ages, this means the great tribulation refers to something bigger than the tribulation that was to befall Jerusalem in just a few years. Although the fall of Jerusalem is a theme of Revelation, the composition of the very global crowd appears to preclude that reading.

They came out of the great tribulation—the church militant—and are those who washed their robes white in the blood of the Lamb. They are now the church triumphant, palm branches in hand. They are before the throne, and the one who sits on the throne dwells among them as Emmanuel. This is plainly the company of the saved. They will not hunger or thirst anymore. The sun shall not beat down on them, or any heat. The Lamb will feed them, and lead them to waters, and God will wipe away every tear.

One more thing should be mentioned, which is that this section of Revelation is rich in references from the prophet Isaiah.

> They shall not hunger nor thirst; Neither shall the heat nor sun smite them: For he that hath mercy on them shall lead them, Even by the springs of water shall he guide them. (Is. 49:10)

> He will swallow up death in victory; And the Lord GOD will wipe away tears from off all faces; And the rebuke

of his people shall he take away from off all the earth: For the Lord hath spoken it. (Is. 25:8)

And the Lord will create upon every dwelling place of mount Zion, And upon her assemblies, A cloud and smoke by day, And the shining of a flaming fire by night: For upon all the glory shall be a defence. And there shall be a tabernacle for a shadow in the daytime from the heat, And for a place of refuge, and for a covert from storm and from rain. (Is. 4:5–6)

In short, this is the language of salvation that applies to all God's people.

CHAPTER 8

THE PRAYERS OF THE SAINTS

> And when he had opened the seventh seal, there was
> silence in heaven about the space of half an hour.
> (Rev. 8:1)

We now come to the seventh and final seal of the scroll. Given the dramatic nature of what happened when the first six were opened, we are expecting some sort of earth shattering explosion when the final seal is broken. But . . . nothing. Nothing but silence.

There are two possible scriptural settings that may be in view here. One is that just a few verses down, an angel is going to offer up incense, and that incense is representative of the prayers of all the saints (Rev. 8:3). These prayers are offered up on the golden altar that is before the throne. A few chapters earlier, when the fifth seal was opened, things were *not* silent in Heaven when the souls under that altar were crying out to the Lord to avenge their blood. Now it appears that an angel has gathered up their prayers and is presenting them as incense, and everything is quiet for that formal presentation.

This appears to match the custom of the Temple. When Zacharias is serving in the Temple, during the time that the incense was being presented, the people were waiting outside quietly, silently praying. "And the whole multitude of the people were praying without at the time of incense" (Luke 1:10). "And the people waited for Zacharias, and marvelled that he tarried so long in the temple" (Luke 1:21). Here an angel is presenting their prayers in the form of incense, and that presentation takes about half an hour.

Another possible allusion is to the siege of Jericho. The opening of the seventh seal here is followed by the blowing of trumpets (Rev. 8:6), which is what happened when the walls of Jericho fell. Not only so, but prior to the blowing of those trumpets, the Israelites marched around that fated city in silence. And so in both instances you have silence > trumpets > conquest of God's enemies.

JUDGMENT IS READY

> And I saw the seven angels which stood before God; and to them were given seven trumpets. And another angel came and stood at the altar, having a golden

censer; and there was given unto him much incense, that he should offer it with the prayers of all saints upon the golden altar which was before the throne. And the smoke of the incense, which came with the prayers of the saints, ascended up before God out of the angel's hand. And the angel took the censer, and filled it with fire of the altar, and cast it into the earth: and there were voices, and thunderings, and light-nings, and an earthquake. And the seven angels which had the seven trumpets prepared themselves to sound. (Rev. 8:2–6)

The seven seals of the scroll have been opened, and we come now to the next round—the seven trumpets. Seven angels stood before God (which would be standing before the throne), and each was given a trumpet (v. 2).

Another angel came, and because His functions at the al-tar are *priestly* in nature, most commentators assume that this is a representation of Christ in another of His offices. Another argument for this is that it would be odd for a mere creature to be presenting the prayers of the saints to God. That is reserved for our great High Priest. Still less would it be appropriate for a mere angel to *answer* those prayers.

At any rate, this angel comes and stands at the altar, carrying a golden censer. He is given much incense, which He mixes with the prayers of the saints, and presents it on the golden altar before the throne (v. 3). The smoke of the incense, mixed together with the prayers of the saints, ascends up to God from the hand of the angel (v. 4). And then, in an obvious answer to prayer, the angel fills up the censer with fire from the altar, and casts it all down upon the earth (v. 5). As a consequence, there was a dramatic impact on the earth—voices, lightning, thunder, and an earthquake (v. 5). With that preliminary judgment completed, the seven other angels prepared themselves to sound their trumpets (v. 6).

The prayers represented here are no doubt the prayers of the martyred saints who were under that same altar back at the fifth seal. They were crying out for vengeance, and were told to be patient for "a little season" (Rev. 6:11). That season of waiting is apparently now complete, and it is time for their prayers to be answered.

Given that the prayers being answered here are prayers from first-century martyrs, we may conclude that this battery of judgment coming from the seven trumpets are judgments that are going to be falling on Jerusalem in the course of the Jewish War (A.D. 66-70).

GREAT TRIBULATION

> The first angel sounded, and there followed hail and fire mingled with blood, and they were cast upon the earth: and the third part of trees was burnt up, and all green grass was burnt up. (Rev. 8:7)

The seven trumpets follow the same general pattern that the seven seals did, with the first four divided from the final three. In this case, the last three trumpets are identified as "woes." With the seals, the first four were associated with horsemen. There is no pressing reason to take all these in a serial fashion, as though we now have a total of fourteen railroad cars or beads on a string. The description is of the apocalyptic destruction of the city of Jerusalem, and each trumpet gives us a fuller picture of what was going to happen in the one cataclysmic judgment that was going to fall upon that wretched city. The symbolic language here is of an exhaustive devastation, but the plain warning of Jesus indicates that these symbols are not overblown when we consider what was actually going to happen to the city and the surrounding territory of Judea.

"Then let them which be *in Judaea* flee into the mountains" (Matt. 24:16).

"For then shall be *great tribulation*, such as was not since the beginning of the world to this time, no, nor ever shall be" (Matt. 24:21).

The sounding of the trumpets signals the commencement of battle—this is God's war against an apostate nation. The combination of hail and fire and blood make us think of the judgment that God rained down upon Egypt (Ex. 9:23; Ps. 18:13; Ps. 78:48; Ps. 105:32). The destruction of Jerusalem occurred in 70 A.D., but there was plenty of devastation to Judea in the years running up to that fateful year. Israel, once gloriously delivered from Egypt, had herself become Egypt.

In this passage, it says that a third of the trees were destroyed. Josephus records that the Romans cut down all the trees around Jerusalem for about ninety furlongs out (with a furlong being 220 yards). Jerusalem was also surrounded with pleasant gardens, which were also wiped out. This was devastation enough, but it is also possible that the grass and the trees represent men (as possibly indicated in Rev. 7:3 and 9:4)—the trees being kings, princes and rulers, and the grass being the ordinary folk. In any case, whether it was one or the other, or both, it was a grim situation.

MOVING MOUNTAINS

> And the second angel sounded, and as it were a great mountain burning with fire was cast into the sea: and the third part of the sea became blood; And the third part of the creatures which were in the sea, and had life, died; and the third part of the ships were destroyed. (Rev. 8:8–9)

The doom predicted by Jesus is falling upon Jerusalem, and these events are fulfilled in the Jewish War of 66-70 A.D. In order for this to become plain to us, we have to begin with how the Bible speaks about such things. Kingdoms are frequently spoken of as "mountains," and the judgments that fall upon them are described with appropriate imagery. We see this both with expressions of faith in times of trouble, and expressions of dismay in times of judgment.

Here is an expression of faith:

"Therefore will not we fear, though the earth be removed, And though *the mountains be carried into the midst of the sea*" (Ps. 46:2; cf. Is. 2:2; Zech. 4:7).

And how is a terrifying judgment against Babylon described?

"Behold, I am against thee, *O destroying mountain*, saith the LORD, Which destroyest all the earth: And I will stretch out mine hand upon thee, and roll thee down from the rocks, *and will make thee a burnt mountain*" (Jer. 51:25).

So we have Old Testament expressions of judgment on nations in terms of mountains being burnt and mountains being thrown into the sea. And recall what happened when Jesus cursed the fig tree—which was a sign of the coming judgment upon *Israel*. What does Jesus say?

> Jesus answered and said unto them, Verily I say unto you, If ye have faith, and doubt not, ye shall not only do this which is done to the fig tree, but also if ye shall say unto *this mountain, Be thou removed, and be thou cast into the sea*; it shall be done. (Matt. 21:21)

What mountain? *This* mountain, the mountain they were standing on, the mountain that the city of Jerusalem was built on (Matt. 21:18). In other words, Jesus cursed the fig tree, representing Israel, and then told His disciples that their authoritative command, delivered in faith, would be the instrument that would cause Jerusalem to be thrown into the sea. Who overthrew Jerusalem? In one sense, the Roman Titus did. But in another sense, Jerusalem was thrown down by the twelve apostles.

That sea probably represents the Gentile nations, as it does throughout Scripture. The image of a mountain city being thrown into the sea is an image of judgment, and is not meant to be taken literally—as though Mount Zion was destined to go whistling overhead. And in the same way, the sea is symbolic of the Gentile world, into which the Jews who survived the war would be dispersed. The burning object, like a mountain, was thrown into the ocean and quenched, and it caused devastation there as well.

There *may* be a literal element in the fulfillment however. Josephus records a battle between the Romans and the Galileans that occurred on the Sea of Galilee. It was a slaughter—"one might see the lake all bloody, and full of dead bodies, for not one of them escaped." The result is not hard to compare to the results of the second trumpet: the "dead bodies all swelled; and as the dead bodies were inflamed by the sun, and putrefied, they corrupted the air . . ." (*Wars* III.10.9).

Jerusalem was cursed. Jerusalem was burned in 70 A.D. Jerusalem was settled on a great mountain. Jerusalem persecuted the apostles as they had done with their Lord. And so the apostles commanded, and it was done.

JUDGED WITH WORMWOOD

> And the third angel sounded, and there fell a great star from heaven, burning as it were a lamp, and it fell upon the third part of the rivers, and upon the fountains of waters; And the name of the star is called Wormwood: and the third part of the waters became wormwood; and many men died of the waters, because they were made bitter. (Rev. 8:10–11)

The seven trumpets are harbingers of a coming judgment upon a wicked and unbelieving city. In the Old Testament, the Canaanite city of Jericho was solemnly sealed in her destruction by seven trumpets blasting. What this indicates is a strong *reversal* theme in Revelation. Here Jerusalem is in the place of Jericho, the chosen people have now taken the place of the pagan Canaanites. The plagues that rain down on Israel in this book are reminiscent of the plagues that wiped out Egypt—and in Rev. 11:8, this is a reversal that is made explicit—Jerusalem is identified with both Sodom *and Egypt*. These are the two great places in the Old Testament best known for the judgment that fell upon them from Heaven. What is that place now? It is Jerusalem.

The same thing is found in our passage itself. When Moses brought the children of Israel away from the Red Sea (Ex. 15:22), they came to a place called Marah. It was called that because the water was bitter. The Lord showed Moses a tree there, which he threw into the bitter water in order to make it sweet (Ex. 15:23-25). In this passage, the reversal is plainly shown—the waters are sweet, and God throws a great star, burning like a torch (reminiscent of the tree in Exodus), into the water in such a way as to make them bitter. Why is this significant? Because *wormwood* means bitter, and because of the warning that was given to them at Marah, with Egypt of recent memory still smoldering.

> And said, If thou wilt diligently hearken to the voice of the LORD thy God, and wilt do that which is right in his sight, and wilt give ear to his commandments, and keep all his statutes, I will put none of these diseases upon thee, *which I have brought upon the Egyptians*: for I am the LORD that healeth thee. (Ex. 15:26)

If they kept his commandments, they would not be visited with the diseases that had afflicted the Egyptians. They would not take the place of Egypt. But unfortunately they did not keep God's commandments, and now He was making Marah bitter again. So keep in mind, once again, that this judgment is aimed straight at *Israel*.

The name of the star is Wormwood, which means bitterness, and the falling star turns the water to wormwood, which still means bitterness. Because of it, men die—either because the water is poisoned, or because they refuse to drink it because it is so bad. And that is what every form of disobedience and idolatry always produces (Dt. 29:18). When they follow after the Baalim, God gives them wormwood to drink (Jer. 9:14-15). Because the prophets are profane, God will feed them with wormwood (Jer. 23:15). This was a signal mark of God's fierce judgments (Lam. 3:15, 19). And in one instance, it was the sin—turning judgment into wormwood—that invites the further judgment from God (Amos 5:6). This was precisely the great sin on the part of the Sanhedrin—that of condemning the Lord Jesus to a cross of wood, where He would be offered vinegar mixed with gall. What was this but the crime of turning justice into wormwood? This is what invited the cataclysmic destruction of 70 A.D.

THE STARS FALL

> And the fourth angel sounded, and the third part of the sun was smitten, and the third part of the moon, and the third part of the stars; so as the third part of them was darkened, and the day shone not for a third part of it, and the night likewise. (Rev. 8:12)

The fourth trumpet is blown, and the visitation comes upon the sun, moon, and stars. The judgment is partial, not total, but it is nonetheless striking. The question raised by the image is this: is the sun, for example, partially eclipsed, with a third of it covered? Or is the light from the entire sun diminished by a third, as could happen with thick air pollution? I take this as symbolic, not literal, but the nature of the picture affects the understanding of what is being pictured. I take this as an indication of political upheaval in and around the time of the Jewish War—during which the Roman emperors Nero, Galba, Otho, and Vitellius all died, and not peacefully in bed either. One after another killed his predecessor. And yet, Rome continued.

Throughout the Old Testament, the language of a collapsing or failing solar system is the language that indicates judgment upon a nation or city. Consider the following (Is. 13:9-11, 19; 24:19-23; 34:4-5; Ezek. 32:7-8, 11-12; Joel 2:10, 28-32; Acts 2:16-21). The sun, moon and stars are representations of earthly rulers, and what is happening to them in the heavenly vision is what is actually going to happen to their counterparts on earth. In this case, the indication is of a partial judgment.

It is at least worth mentioning that later in the book, the dragon (who is the devil) dragged down a third of the stars with his tail (Rev. 12:4).

WOES IN THE OFFING

And I beheld, and heard an angel flying through the midst of heaven, saying with a loud voice, Woe, woe,

woe, to the inhabiters of the earth by reason of the
other voices of the trumpet of the three angels, which
are yet to sound! (Rev. 8:13)

Just as the first four seals were set off from the last three
(by the device of having the first four as the four horsemen), so also the seven trumpets are divided into four followed by three. The first four appear to be warning judgments, with the last three, each one called a woe, being the
culmination or fulfillment of that judgment.

Given the context of judgment falling upon the city of
Jerusalem, it is best to take the first woe as the internal
strife among the Jewish rebels, the second as the besieging
of the city by the Romans, and the third as the fiery overthrow of the city.

But before the woes come, the woes are announced beforehand, which is the point of this text. The King James
and New King James tell us that the messenger was an
angel. But there is some variation in the manuscripts—the
ESV and the NASB state that an *eagle* is the one making the
announcement. Interestingly, the Vulgate has *aquila* at this
place—an eagle.

If we take it as an angel, we see that the last three trumpets are grim enough to require their own introduction. If
the messenger is an eagle, we should remember that eagles are carrion birds, and in the toppling of Jerusalem, a
million Jews were going to die. This is a common image in
the Old Testament (Dt. 28:49; Jer. 4:13; Lam 4:19; Hos.
8:1; Hab. 1:8; Matt. 24:28). The image here is the swift-
ness of the eagle, but the reference from Habakkuk shows

that the eagles fly fast in their hunger. "They shall fly as the eagle that hasteth to eat." And the covenant judgment of being devoured by the birds of the air is also common (Dt. 28:26; Prov. 30:17; Rev. 19:17-18).

In either case, the messenger is telling the inhabitants of the land to brace themselves.

CHAPTER 9

DEMONS ARRIVE

And the fifth angel sounded, and I saw a star fall from heaven unto the earth: and to him was given the key of the bottomless pit. And he opened the bottomless pit; and there arose a smoke out of the pit, as the smoke of a great furnace; and the sun and the air were darkened by reason of the smoke of the pit. And there came out of the smoke locusts upon the earth: and unto them was given power, as the scorpions of the earth have power. And it was commanded them that they should not hurt the grass of the earth, neither any green thing, neither any tree; but only those men

> which have not the seal of God in their foreheads. And
> to them it was given that they should not kill them,
> but that they should be tormented five months: and
> their torment was as the torment of a scorpion, when
> he striketh a man. And in those days shall men seek
> death, and shall not find it; and shall desire to die, and
> death shall flee from them. (Rev. 9:1–6)

So the fifth angel sounds, and the first of three woes is de-clared. In order to understand this well, we have to review some of our history.

The Jewish War lasted for three and a half years. This was prophetically declared by John the apostle just a few chapters later. The Temple is measured, and it is declared that the Gentiles will trample the holy city for forty-two months (Rev. 11:2). And the same figure is given in the next verse, under a different form. forty-two months of thirty days each amounts to 1260 days. In this passage, we are given the tormenting figure of five months, which I would link to the final months of the siege of Jerusalem (April through August, A.D. 70). This was the time during which the Jewish defenders of the city turned on each oth-er in a terrible frenzy, and which Josephus records in his annals (*Wars* 5.1.5, 5.10.5, 6.3.4-5). Why is this relevant?

A star falls from heaven, and because a personal pronoun is used, we know that it is a person. He opens the Abyss, and smoke comes out of it, blocking the sun and choking the air. Out of that smoke a horde of locusts comes, only with power to sting like scorpions. I take these to be de-mons because of the Lord's instruction elsewhere. In the exorcism of Legion, the demons beg not to be sent to the *Abyss*, same word (Luke 8:31). And the Lord says something quite striking when He tells us what happens when a demon is cast out of a man.

"When the unclean spirit is gone out of a man, *he walketh through dry places*, seeking rest, and findeth none. Then he saith, I will return into my house from whence I came out; and when he is come, he findeth it empty, swept, and garnished. Then goeth he, and taketh with himself seven other spirits more wicked than himself, and they enter in and dwell there: and the last state of that man is worse than the first. *Even so shall it be also unto this wicked generation*" (Matt. 12:43–45).

Jesus had spent three years casting demons out of the House of Israel. Israel was the house that was found empty, swept, and garnished. All the demons that had been cast out—and there had been a multitude—went and gathered up a host of more demons, like a plague of locusts with a sting, and they poured back into that wicked generation. The Jewish defenders of Jerusalem in the final months were demon-possessed, hell bent on destruction. As we shall see in the next verses, they had a king over them, with the Hebrew name of *Abaddon* and the Greek name of *Apollyon*, which both mean *destruction*.

The demons pent up in the Abyss are beyond frustrated because their nature is to destroy, and they dwell in a place where everything is already destroyed. They cannot wreck because they live in a wrecked place.

When released, they do not hurt the grass, and they cannot touch those who were sealed in chapter seven. Those they torment long for death, but death still eludes them.

THE FIRST WOE: INTERNAL STRIFE

> And the shapes of the locusts were like unto horses prepared unto battle; and on their heads were as it were crowns like gold, and their faces were as the faces of men. And they had hair as the hair of women, and their teeth were as the teeth of lions. And they had breastplates, as it were breastplates of iron; and the sound of their wings was as the sound of chariots of many horses running to battle. And they had tails like unto scorpions, and there were stings in their tails: and their power was to hurt men five months. And they had a king over them, which is the angel of the bottomless pit, whose name in the Hebrew tongue is Abaddon, but in the Greek tongue hath his name Apollyon. One woe is past; and, behold, there come two woes more hereafter. (Rev. 9:7–12)

These demonic locust-like creatures were released from the Abyss, but they are not like actual locusts in certain key respects. I take them for demons, released to wreak havoc in the streets of Jerusalem during the last five months of the siege. They are *like* locusts, but there are differences. First, actual locusts devour the greenery, but the grass, the trees, and every green thing are protected from them. Second, their macabre appearance indicates intelligence (men's faces), effeminate transvestitism (women's hair), apparent invulnerability (iron breastplates), real ferocity (lions' teeth), and venomous malice (scorpion-like sting in the tail). And third, these creatures had a king (v. 11), while locusts have no king: "The locusts have no king, Yet go they forth all of them by bands" (Prov. 30:27).

The demons imparted their characteristics to the men they came to possess, the demon-possessed tribe of Jerusalem's defenders. Just as a deaf and dumb spirit results in a deaf and dumb *man*, and an unclean spirit results in an unclean *man*, dwelling among the tombs, so also this bizarre demon army created a vile army within the holy city. The demons descended, not upon the green things, and not upon the servants of God who had His mark, but on the men without such a mark.

Here is part of Josephus' description of what happened then:

> With their insatiable hunger for loot, they ransacked the houses of the wealthy, murdered men and violated women for sport; they drank their spoils with blood, and from mere satiety and shamelessness gave themselves up to effeminate practices, plaiting their hair and putting on women's clothes, drenched themselves with perfumes and painting their eyelids to make themselves attractive. They copied not merely the dress, but also the passions of women, devising in their excess of licentiousness unlawful pleasures in which they wallowed as in a brothel. Thus they entirely polluted the city with their foul practices. Yet though they wore women's faces, their hands were

murderous. They would approach with mincing steps, then suddenly become fighting men, and, whipping out their swords from under their dyed cloaks, they would run through every passerby. (*Wars* 4.9.10)

Their authority could be flexed, and was, but it was a spurious authority. They wore crowns, but the crowns were not genuine gold, but made of something that *looked* like gold. This passage is the only one in Revelation where the word *stephanos*, the word for *crown*, is used for the ungodly.

All of this is beyond horrific, and it is still just the first woe.

ON SCHEDULE

And the sixth angel sounded, and I heard a voice from the four horns of the golden altar which is before God, Saying to the sixth angel which had the trumpet, Loose the four angels which are bound in the great river Euphrates. And the four angels were loosed, which were prepared for an hour, and a day, and a month, and a year, for to slay the third part of men. (Rev. 9:13–15)

When the sixth angel sounded his trumpet, the Roman legions were released, described here under the figure of four angels of destruction. A voice came from the four horns of the gold altar, which means that the command for this to happen now was all within the divine order and plan. Remember that the martyred saints had prayed from this same altar, and now their prayer is being answered (8:3). God's answer was already prepared. That is what we see in v. 15 also—the angels of destruction that were loosed had been prepared down to the minute. They were released then, at that moment in history, and not before. This was a scheduled event, a timed event (Dan. 9:24-26). They were prepared for the hour, the day, the month, and the year. This was no accident, no happenstance.

They were released to come across the Euphrates, which was the northeast border of the Promised Land. The 10th Legion, part of the destroying force, had been located on the Euphrates. Josephus records the Roman presence there (*Wars* 7.1.3). This had long been a troublesome border for the Jews—the Assyrians had come across it, as had the Babylonians, and the Persians. Now the Romans. The number of the invading army is translated literally as 200 million (v. 16), but the Greek is *myriads of myriads*. As Larry Ball points out, this is like our number *gazillion*. An innumerable host swarmed in to surround Jerusalem.[1]

And all this fits with what Jesus had predicted would happen, and all within one generation. "Verily I say unto you, This generation shall not pass, till all these things be fulfilled" (Matt. 24:34). Not only so, but Jesus had also taught us that the destruction of Jerusalem was one of the central themes of all Old Testament prophecy—meaning that the apocalyptic imagery that John uses for it in Revelation is hardly overdone. "For these be the days of vengeance, *that all things which are written may be fulfilled*" (Luke 21:22).

---

1. Larry Ball, *Blessed Is He Who Reads* (Fountain Inn, SC: Victorious Hope Publishing, 2015), 150-154.

COUNTLESS HORSES

> And the number of the army of the horsemen were two hundred thousand thousand: and I heard the number of them. And thus I saw the horses in the vision, and them that sat on them, having breastplates of fire, and of jacinth, and brimstone: and the heads of the horses were as the heads of lions; and out of their mouths issued fire and smoke and brimstone. By these three was the third part of men killed, by the fire, and by the smoke, and by the brimstone, which issued out of their mouths. For their power is in their mouth, and in their tails: for their tails were like unto serpents, and had heads, and with them they do hurt. (Rev. 9:16–19)

As mentioned earlier, the invading army consisted of "myriads of myriads," symbolizing a staggering number. As happened earlier with the 144,000, John first *heard* the number and then he turned and *saw*. This is not simply a marching army of incredible size, but is a cavalry of mounted warriors. If taken literally, the number would be 200 million.

The cavalrymen were decked out colorfully with breastplates of fiery red, sapphire blue, and sulfur yellow. The horses were like nothing on earth, having lion heads that breathed out fire, smoke, and sulfur, a breath that had the power to kill a third part of all the men. This destructive breath appears to match the colors of their riders: fire red, blue smoke, and sulfur yellow. The horses had lion heads

that breathed calamity, and their tails were headed ser-
pents, with a venomous bite.

This is all connected to the sixth trumpet, the middle of
the last three trumpets. We are not yet at the horrifying
end of the Battle of Jerusalem. We are still in the build-up
to that climax.

GLAD TO BE IN HELL

> And the rest of the men which were not killed by these
> plagues yet repented not of the works of their hands,
> that they should not worship devils, and idols of gold,
> and silver, and brass, and stone, and of wood: which
> neither can see, nor hear, nor walk: Neither repent-
> ed they of their murders, nor of their sorceries, nor of
> their fornication, nor of their thefts. (Rev. 9:20–21)

We sometimes like to imagine that the damned in Hell
would gladly repent, if only given the ghost of a chance.
But yet here we have a harbinger of Hell, a hell-on-earth,
and though you might think that would be an inducement
to repentance, it turns out that repentance is a gift of the
sovereign God. There really is a mystery to lawlessness; it
is a rebellion that makes no sense whatever.

The survivors of the previous plagues should have taken
the fierce reality of those plagues into account—but did
not. Notice that it says they refused to repent of the works
of their own hands. They crafted their own sinfulness; it
was handmade idolatry. This is another place in the New
Testament where idolatry and devil worship go together.
"But I say, that the things which the Gentiles sacrifice, they

sacrifice to devils, and not to God: and I would not that ye should have fellowship with devils" (1 Cor. 10:20). Sacrificing to idols is sacrificing to demons, and sacrificing to demons is having *koinonia*-fellowship with demons.

The material that is used to fashion the idols can vary—gold, silver, brass, stone, or wood—but the immaterial substance being invoked is always the same, which is devilish and demonic. John tells us that these idols are made from many different materials, but it does not matter. None of them are alive. They cannot see, hear, or walk. And because those who make them have become like unto them (Ps. 115:4-8), it follows that these idolaters cannot see, hear, or walk either.

In what sense? They cannot see righteousness, they cannot hear righteous commands, and they cannot walk in righteousness. There is the idol in the material world, gold, silver, and so on. Then there is the spiritual idol behind the matter, which is the demon. And there is also the invisible idol in the idolaters' hearts—the things they would have to surrender were they to repent. And these sins include murder, sorcery, fornication, and thievery. These heart sins are their "precious," and they will not let them go. The sinners will not let the sin go, and the sins will not let the sinners go.

Remember that the bloodguilt of murder would include the bloodguilt of abortion, a sin common in the first century as it is in ours. The word for sorcery is *pharmakeia*, from which we get the word *pharmacy*. The occultism here is related to drug use, and when drug use becomes rampant, occultism is never far behind. Fornication would include the same kind of corrupt desires that we celebrate on the

Internet. And they governed their lives with thievery in their hearts, just as we do. And Scripture teaches that having your world collapse around you will not by itself bring repentance. In order for that to happen, the gift of God must be given (Acts 5:31; 2 Tim. 2:25).

CHAPTER 10

A FEW THINGS ARE SEALED

And I saw another mighty angel come down from heaven, clothed with a cloud: and a rainbow was upon his head, and his face was as it were the sun, and his feet as pillars of fire: And he had in his hand a little book open: and he set his right foot upon the sea, and his left foot on the earth, And cried with a loud voice, as when a lion roareth: and when he had cried, seven thunders uttered their voices. And when the seven thunders had uttered their voices, I was about to write: and I heard a voice from heaven saying unto me, Seal

up those things which the seven thunders uttered, and
write them not. (Rev. 10:1–4)

Between the sounding of the sixth and seventh trumpet,
we have an interlude—in the same way that we had an interlude between the opening of the sixth and seventh seals
in chapter seven.

It appears that the "mighty angel" that descends at this
point should be identified as the Lord Jesus Himself. Here
are some of the reasons. His appearance is consistent with
how the Lord is described earlier in Revelation—face shining like the sun (Rev. 1:16), feet like brass burning as in a
furnace (Rev. 1:15), and the rainbow that is now around
His head was earlier around His throne (Rev. 4:3). He is
clothed with a cloud, and that is new, but the Lord does
appear on a cloud later (Rev. 14:14). The one sound argument that this is not the Lord comes from the fact that it
is not mentioned here that John worships Him as he did
earlier (Rev. 1:17).

The Lord was the only one who could open the sealed
book earlier, and here the mighty angel holds a little book,
one that is already open. He has one foot on the sea and
the other on the earth, indicating His authority over the
entire globe. It also may indicate that He is speaking to
Jew and Gentile both—the Jews being the land and the
Gentiles represented by the sea.

Another indication that this is the Lord can be found in
the allusions to Psalm 29. The thunders are the result of
the angel's loud voice, indicating that this is the voice of
the Lord. "The voice of the LORD is upon the waters: The

God of glory thundereth: The LORD is upon many waters" (Psalm 29:3).

The opened book is little, small enough for John to eat. The contents of the book have *largely* been unsealed, with the events contained in it accomplished for the most part. But at the same time, John is told *not* to write down what the seven thunders said. This is an indication that some things revealed to John were not to be fulfilled until later—a time outside the scope of the book. While the bulk of what John saw was fulfilled in the first century, there was some reserved for later.

For example, John is told later not to seal up the book of his Revelation, because the time was upon them (Rev. 22:10). Centuries before, Daniel had been told to seal up the words because the fulfillment was a long way out (Dan. 12:4). It would be odd for God to tell Daniel this, when the fulfillment was four centuries away, and for Him to tell John the opposite when the fulfillment of his words would be over twenty centuries away. But here, what the thunders said has been withheld from us.

THE END OF AN ERA

And the angel which I saw stand upon the sea and upon the earth lifted up his hand to heaven, And sware by him that liveth for ever and ever, who created heaven, and the things that therein are, and the earth, and the things that therein are, and the sea, and the things which are therein, that there should be time no longer: But in the days of the voice of the seventh angel, when

he shall begin to sound, the mystery of God should be
finished, as he hath declared to his servants the prophets. (Revelation 10:5–7)

We have identified this mighty angel with the Lord Jesus.
He stands over the world, with His right foot on the sea
and the other on the earth. He has the little book open in
His hand. In this passage, He lifts up His hand to heaven
in order to swear, in order to take an oath. This should
resolve forever the question of whether it is lawful for believers to swear.

He swore in the name of the one who lives forever, the
one who created heaven and everything in it, along with
the earth and everything in it, and along with the sea and
everything in it. That was the basis of His oath. What was
the *content* of the oath?

He swore that there would be no more delay. The souls
under the altar had been told to be patient for just a little
while longer. They would have to be patient no more—the
time has come. When the seventh angel sounds his trumpet, *everything* would be complete.

But what does that mean? There are two things ex-
pressed about this fulfillment. It is described as the "mystery of God," and it was a mystery that had been declared
beforehand to His servants the prophets. This gives us the
content of the mystery plainly. Where the Scripture uses
this phrase elsewhere, it is talking about the fashioning of
one new kind of man—Christian—out of the old categories
of Jew and Gentile.

Now to him that is of power to stablish you according to my gospel, and the preaching of Jesus Christ, according to *the revelation of the mystery*, which was kept secret since the world began. (Rom. 16:25)

That their hearts might be comforted, being knit together in love, and unto all riches of the full assurance of understanding, to *the acknowledgment of the mystery of God*, and of the Father, and of Christ. (Col. 2:2)

How that by revelation he made known unto me *the mystery*; (as I wrote afore in few words, Whereby, when ye read, ye may understand my knowledge in *the mystery of Christ*) Which in other ages was not made known unto the sons of men, as it is now revealed unto his holy apostles and prophets by the Spirit; That the Gentiles should be fellowheirs, and of the same body, and partakers of his promise in Christ by the gospel. (Eph. 3:3–6)

The mystery, given to the prophets down through the ages, but now unpacked and made manifest through the gospel, is that Gentiles are going to be made fellow heirs together with Jews.

This is all very well, but what does all that have to do with the seventh angel blowing his trumpet? The answer is that as long as the Temple in Jerusalem stood, there would be standing pressure for the Gentiles to become Jews as part of becoming Christian. This was the great controversy of the first generation in the church, and that controversy would continue as long as the Temple continued. The dominant identity of the church was going to be Jewish as long as the Temple remained.

When the seventh angel sounded, Jerusalem was done.

THE CHANGING OF THE WORLD

> And the voice which I heard from heaven spake unto me again, and said, Go and take the little book which is open in the hand of the angel which standeth upon the sea and upon the earth. And I went unto the angel, and said unto him, Give me the little book. And he said unto me, Take it, and eat it up; and it shall make thy belly bitter, but it shall be in thy mouth sweet as honey. And I took the little book out of the angel's hand, and ate it up; and it was in my mouth sweet as honey: and as soon as I had eaten it, my belly was bitter. And he said unto me, Thou must prophesy again before many peoples, and nations, and tongues, and kings. (Rev. 10:8–11)

John hears a voice from heaven again, which instructs him to go up to the angel who is straddling earth and sea. When he gets there, he is supposed to take the little open book from the hand of the great angel. And so John obediently approached the angel and said, "Give me the little book." Given that the angel was immense, the fact that John could take the book and eat it means that it must have truly been tiny compared to the size of the angel.

What happens here is a precise parallel to what happened to Ezekiel. That ancient prophet was addressing the destruction of Jerusalem (also), as accomplished by the Babylonians in 586 B.C.

> Moreover he said unto me, Son of man, eat that thou findest; eat this roll, and go speak unto the house of Israel. So I opened my mouth, and he caused me to eat that roll. And he said unto me, Son of man, cause thy belly to eat, and fill thy bowels with this roll that I give thee. Then did I eat it; and it was in my mouth as honey for sweetness. (Ezek. 3:1–3)

The bitterness that John experienced is mentioned a few verses later in Ezekiel.

"So the spirit lifted me up, and took me away, and I went in bitterness, in the heat of my spirit; but the hand of the LORD was strong upon me" (Ezek. 3:14).

This combination of sweetness and bitterness means that a message of judgment must be *both*. The sweetness lies in the vindication of God's servants. The martyrs under the altar will have their prayer answered. The persecutors will be utterly thrown down. Justice will be done, and the saints of God will say *hallelujah*. The only time that word is used in the New Testament is some chapters ahead of us in Revelation, when the saints exult in the fact that the smoke of Babylon ascends forever and ever (Rev. 19:3). But at the same time, we remember (also from Ezekiel) that considered in isolation, God takes no pleasure in the death of the wicked (Ezek. 33:11). As a stand-alone reality, the stubborn willfulness of the rebel is a genuine tragedy. It is not a tragedy that God will allow them to use in order to emotionally blackmail those who do rejoice in the will of God, but it is a tragedy nonetheless.

We see in this passage that John is not just a simple observer. He is told that eating the book, tasting its sweetness, and having his stomach turned by the bitter results of the message, means that he, John, must prophesy *again*. This book eaten means that John is the prophet.

The book of Revelation continues as a condemnation of the city of Jerusalem, but we see here that the fall of the old system has ramifications for the whole world—the message is for "many peoples, nations, and tongues, and kings." And this what the destruction of Jerusalem would facilitate—a gospel for the whole world.

Remember that the book of Revelation has three sets of seven. We have seven seals, seven trumpets, and seven bowls. There had been an interlude before the seventh seal was opened, and we are in the midst of a second interlude now, right before the blowing of the seventh trumpet. Before the hammer falls, there is a divine pause, the witnesses confirm their testimony, and then the judgment.

CHAPTER 11

TREADING DOWN THE SANCTUARY

> And there was given me a reed like unto a rod: and the
> angel stood, saying, Rise, and measure the temple of
> God, and the altar, and them that worship therein. But
> the court which is without the temple leave out, and
> measure it not; for it is given unto the Gentiles: and
> the holy city shall they tread under foot forty and two
> months. (Rev. 11:1–2)

John is given a reed to use in measuring, and the first thing
we should think of is how a man is given a measuring rod in
Ezekiel (40-47) to measure the Temple in the vision there.
John is told to measure three things—the Holy of Holies

(the word is *naos*), the altar, and those who worship there. This measuring is a device for indicating separation, dividing those who will be protected in the calamity to come from those who will not be protected. The measuring is intended to mark out those who are genuine worshipers of God.

But John is told *not* to measure outside the Temple. This is a curious expression because the open court outside the Temple was specifically named the Court of the Gentiles. The way the Jewish hierarchy had set up a market there for selling clean animals (which represented the Jews), thereby supplanting Gentiles, was one of the charges Jesus had leveled against them when He cleansed the Temple. "And he taught, saying unto them, Is it not written, My house shall be called *of all nations* the house of prayer? but ye have made it a den of thieves" (Mark 11:17). And when Solomon had dedicated the Temple, he had specifically carved out a place for Gentiles (1 Kings 8:41-43). It was given over to them in this judgment, but it was a place that should have been theirs all along.

The measuring indicated that true Jews and false Jews were going to be distinguished in the judgment that was about to fall. The outer court was going to be turned over to the Gentiles (to whom it belonged), and *their* time to be measured was not yet. That would come.

"And they shall fall by the edge of the sword, and shall be led away captive into all nations: and Jerusalem shall be trodden down of the Gentiles, until the times of the Gentiles be fulfilled" (Luke 21:24).

Another important clue is given to us in these verses. The Gentiles will trample on the holy city for forty-two months.

This is a time period familiar to readers of Scripture, and in this section of Revelation it is referred to in three different ways. It is called "forty-two months," "twelve hundred and sixty days," and "a time, times, and half a time." In short, we are talking about three and half years. This is the time that Daniel had said that Antiochus Epiphanes would defile the Temple (Dan. 7:25). It is how long Elijah was used to bring about a drought in Israel (1 Kings 17-18; Jas. 5:17). And this mention kicks off a flurry of references in Revelation. The Gentiles will tread down Jerusalem for this time (Rev. 11:2). The two witnesses will testify for this period of time (Rev. 11:3). The woman pursued by the dragon is chased for this time (Rev. 12:6, 14). The beast will blaspheme for this long (Rev. 13:5).

This is an important time anchor for us, one that will help us unravel what John is talking about. After Nero had a big part of the city of Rome burned, suspicion that he was behind it fell on him. He deflected it by blaming the Christians, and so the first Roman persecution broke out—in November of A.D. 64. That persecution ended when Nero was forced to commit suicide in a coup, which happened in June A.D. 68. This was forty-two months later. The first great persecution of the saints by Rome happened in fulfillment of John's words. And there is another possible fulfillment. While the overlap was not complete, there was *some* overlap. The war between Jerusalem and Rome also lasted for approximately that same period of time.

This interlude between the sixth and seventh trumpets is a pause before the calamitous judgment of A.D. 70 falls upon Jerusalem.

THE TESTIMONY OF THE WITNESSES

> And I will give power unto my two witnesses, and they shall prophesy a thousand two hundred and three-score days, clothed in sackcloth. These are the two olive trees, and the two candlesticks standing before the God of the earth. And if any man will hurt them, fire proceedeth out of their mouth, and devoureth their enemies: and if any man will hurt them, he must in this manner be killed. These have power to shut heaven, that it rain not in the days of their prophecy: and have power over waters to turn them to blood, and to smite the earth with all plagues, as often as they will. (Rev. 11:3–6)

Biblical law requires at least two witnesses before a condemnation, and here, before Jerusalem is finally condemned, the requisite two witnesses are brought forward. The identity of these witnesses has long been disputed and discussed, and this contribution to the discussion is offered with that awareness.

That said, I take these witnesses to represent all the prophets of Israel. The Lord taught us that the guilt of the old covenant era was cumulative. "From the blood of Abel unto the blood of Zacharias, which perished between the altar and the temple: verily I say unto you, It shall be required of this generation" (Luke 11:51). The Lord said this, speaking of the destruction of Jerusalem, which is our topic here. The two witnesses are dressed in sackcloth, which denotes a message of woe and the need for repentance. That matches the narrative as well.

The two witnesses have miraculous powers, as did the prophets of old, and their powers echo the powers of Moses and Elijah, the two who visited with the Lord on the Mount of Transfiguration. Moses turned water to blood, and he struck the earth with all manner of plagues. Elijah called down fire from the sky that consumed the men who had come to arrest him, and he shut up the heavens so that a fierce drought came upon Ahab's Israel. Moses and Elijah also represent for us the Law and the Prophets.

In addition, the two olive trees and two candlesticks are intended to make us think of Zerubbabel and Joshua (Zech. 4:2-14). These two men were true servants of God, serving Him in the civil and religious spheres respectively. In the same way, throughout the Old Testament not only did prophets come out of the wilderness, like Elijah, but they also wielded civic, political power, like Moses and David. And all of them, considered together, were ignored by the establishment in Jerusalem. Their works of power were ignored, and their powerful words were ignored. "Wherefore thus saith the LORD God of hosts, Because ye speak this word, behold, I will make my words in thy mouth fire, and this people wood, and it shall devour them" (Jer. 5:14).

These two men prophesy for 1,260 days, the same period of time that sees the holy city trampled on by the Gentiles. I take this as a picture of the final prophetic culmination. "And he said unto him, If they hear not Moses and the prophets, neither will they be persuaded, though one rose from the dead" (Luke 16:31). They were not persuaded when Jesus rose, as the prophets had said, and neither were they persuaded when they died . . . also as the prophets had said.

DIVORCING ISRAEL

> And when they shall have finished their testimony, the beast that ascendeth out of the bottomless pit shall make war against them, and shall overcome them, and kill them. And their dead bodies shall lie in the street of the great city, which spiritually is called Sodom and Egypt, where also our Lord was crucified. And they of the people and kindreds and tongues and nations shall see their dead bodies three days and an half, and shall not suffer their dead bodies to be put in graves. And they that dwell upon the earth shall rejoice over them, and make merry, and shall send gifts one to another; because these two prophets tormented them that dwelt on the earth. (Rev. 11:7–10)

We now have the first mention of a beast in Revelation. In Scripture, beasts are persecuting political powers. In the popular mind, the beast and the antichrist are the same nefarious figure at the end of the world—but they are really quite distinct. A modern beast would be a figure like Stalin or Mao. A modern antichrist would be a false teacher . . . a mild liberal theologian who denies the Incarnation.

This beast ascends out of the Abyss, showing that his political force and authority are given to him by the underworld. He attacks the two witnesses, but is only allowed to do this *after* they have "finished their testimony." With regard to the preceding verses, I argued that these were not two literal witnesses, but rather represented the chain of prophets throughout the Old Testament era. They came in the spirit and power of Moses and Elijah. Part of the reason for not taking them as two literal prophets can be found in the wording of this section. First, it says that the beast "makes war" against them. This is an odd expression if we are talking about two men. Wars occur between armies. And second, in verses 8-9, the expression *their dead bodies* occurs three times. In the first two of these instances, the literal expression is singular—*their dead body*. This would indicate some sort of corporate body.

They testify for a long time—three and a half years. Their enemies exult over their dead bodies for a short time—three and a half days. The city where they died is identified as Jerusalem—where the Lord was crucified. Jerusalem is the graveyard of prophets. "O Jerusalem, Jerusalem, thou that killest the prophets, and stonest them which are sent unto thee" (Matt. 23:37a). But graveyard is not quite the right expression because in this instance the malevolence of the God-haters is seen in how they deny burial to the witnesses, and how they rejoice and make merry over their death.

The book of Revelation is about the divorce and final putting away of Jerusalem. God's rejection of her can be seen in the language used. This city, the city where Jesus was crucified, can be identified with her true spiritual names—that is, Sodom and Egypt. The once beautiful city had not just undergone mission drift, but rather mission reversal. The people of God had become the anti-people of God. Israel is identified with Sodom in the Old Testament

(Is. 1:10). And here in Revelation, the plagues of Egypt were rained down upon Israel (Rev. 8:6-12; 16:2-12).

Spite and vindictiveness are the hallmark of persecutors. They would not allow the witnesses to be buried, and they rejoiced over their carcasses. Unfortunately, this kind of malice has not been unknown in the history of the church. The ashes of Huss were thrown in the Lake of Constance. The bones of Wycliff were dug up and thrown into the river. The book of Revelation was largely fulfilled in the first century, but the fundamental spiritual realities have not changed.

THE SECOND WOE: THE SIEGE

> And after three days and an half the Spirit of life from God entered into them, and they stood upon their feet; and great fear fell upon them which saw them. And they heard a great voice from heaven saying unto them, Come up hither. And they ascended up to heaven in a cloud; and their enemies beheld them. And the same hour was there a great earthquake, and the tenth part of the city fell, and in the earthquake were slain of men seven thousand: and the remnant were affrighted, and gave glory to the God of heaven. The second woe is past; and, behold, the third woe cometh quickly. (Rev. 11:11–14)

We have surmised that the two witnesses are the totality of the prophetic witness throughout the Old Testament, and in this passage we see their final vindication. Their witness extended from Abel down to Christ. The attempt was made to extinguish their witness, and it appeared as though evil had triumphed. The ungodly had rejoiced at their defeat, but now they stood up on their feet, and the wicked were thrown into great consternation.

They had conducted their witness before the God of the earth (Rev. 11:4). They are here vindicated by the God of heaven (Rev. 11:13). Once again we have testimony to the truth that God loves cliffhangers. He loves to bring the stories He tells to the point of eucatastrophe. The Spirit of life from God entered into them, and their complete defeat was transformed into a complete victory.

When they stood, a great voice from Heaven invited them to ascend, which they did in a cloud. Their enemies saw all of this. What the great voice did was say the same thing that the voice like a trumpet had said to John earlier (Rev. 4:1).

At that same time, there was a great earthquake, which killed seven thousand men. This is a mirror image of what had happened in Elijah's time—when seven thousand had been kept back from idolatry. Here seven thousand were slain for their idolatry. The number is likely symbolic, with seven representing completeness and one thousand representing multitudes.

Now this is not the final destruction of Jerusalem, that which happened in 70 A.D. We are talking here about the first siege of Jerusalem under Cestius. At the same time, the final destruction is still in view because God takes a tithe of the city. The tithe is not a partial payment for God, but rather is testimony to the fact that *all* of it is His. The entire city was dedicated to destruction. Immediately after this down payment, the population was frightened and gave glory to the God of Heaven. This was apparently not true repentance—otherwise the final outcome would have been different.

Josephus records some of the infighting that occurred in Jerusalem in the aftermath of an earthquake—the Idumeans together with the Zealots were able to make an entry into the city because of an earthquake, and then perpetrated a great slaughter.

This completed the second woe. The third was right on top of them.

ANYTIME, ANYWHERE

> And the seventh angel sounded; and there were great voices in heaven, saying, The kingdoms of this world are become the kingdoms of our Lord, and of his Christ; and he shall reign for ever and ever. And the four and twenty elders, which sat before God on their seats, fell upon their faces, and worshipped God, Saying, We give thee thanks, O Lord God Almighty, which art, and wast, and art to come; because thou hast taken to thee thy great power, and hast reigned. And the nations were angry, and thy wrath is come, and the time of the dead, that they should be judged, and that thou shouldest give reward unto thy servants the prophets, and to the saints, and them that fear thy name, small and great; and shouldest destroy them which destroy the earth. And the temple of God was opened in heaven, and there was seen in his temple

the ark of his testament: and there were lightnings, and voices, and thunderings, and an earthquake, and great hail. (Rev. 11:15–19)

The seventh angel blew the seventh trumpet, and the signification of this trumpet blast is declared in heaven by "great voices." It is fitting that the declaration that follows instantly evokes that great musical theme that Handel assigned to it in *The Messiah*—music indeed worthy of great voices. The seventh trumpet indicates the formal establishment of Daniel's fifth kingdom, the rock that struck Nebuchadnezzar's great statue on the feet, and which then grew to become a mountain that filled the entire earth.

The seventh trumpet indicates the formal inauguration of Christ's reign on earth. Christ had ascended into the heavenly places forty years before, and had approached the Ancient of Days on the clouds of heaven (Dan. 7:13), where He was granted universal dominion. "And there was given him dominion, and glory, and a kingdom, that all people, nations, and languages, should serve him: his dominion is an everlasting dominion, which shall not pass away, and his kingdom that which shall not be destroyed" (Dan. 7:14).

But in order for this heavenly kingdom to have its earthly reality made manifest, two great things had to happen. The first is that the Spirit had to be poured out on the church, so that we could do the work of the kingdom in the power and authority of Christ. In order to function as Christ's body on earth, we needed the Spirit to empower us. The second thing that had to happen was the removal of the old Judaic Temple. Before the Christian faith could become the holy Temple of God on the earth, the old shadow had to be removed. Had it remained, it would have been too great a distraction. "In that he saith, A new covenant, he hath made the first old. *Now that which decayeth and waxeth old is ready to vanish away*" (Heb. 8:13).

We saw back in chapter four that the twenty-four elders are representative of all God's elect throughout history. They are the ones who fall on their faces and give glory to God. They worshiped the Almighty, the one who gathered great power to Himself in order to reign. The lament of the saints under the altar in chapter six is now heard. The nations were angry, but God's wrath came upon them. This passage says that it was the "time of the dead," which I do not take as the last judgment at the end of history. Rather, the lament of the saints had earlier asked how long God would delay His judgment, how long before He avenged their blood. The same word for judgment is used here— and this is the point where God gives His reward to His servants the prophets, and to the saints, and to those who feared His name, whether small or great. God would destroy those who destroyed the earth, and a new aeon, the Christian aeon, opened up.

The shadow Temple on earth was flattened so that the Temple in the heavens could be opened up to all mankind. "The temple of God was opened in heaven." And just as the veil hiding the Ark of the Covenant was torn in two when Jesus died, so also the veil of the heavenly curtain was rent. The "ark of his testament" in the celestial realms was now seen. It is no longer hidden away. The mercy seat, the heavenly mercy seat, is no longer hidden in darkness for most of the year. The gospel of the new creation can be preached anytime, anywhere.

And to underscore and emphasize all of this, God italicized this great declaration, and He did it with *lightnings, and voices, and thunderings, and an earthquake, and great hail.*

CHAPTER 12

SATAN ATTACKS

And there appeared a great wonder in heaven; a woman clothed with the sun, and the moon under her feet, and upon her head a crown of twelve stars: And she being with child cried, travailing in birth, and pained to be delivered. And there appeared another wonder in heaven; and behold a great red dragon, having seven heads and ten horns, and seven crowns upon his heads. And his tail drew the third part of the stars of heaven, and did cast them to the earth: and the dragon stood before the woman which was ready to be delivered, for to devour her child as soon as it was born.

And she brought forth a man child, who was to rule all
nations with a rod of iron: and her child was caught
up unto God, and to his throne. And the woman fled
into the wilderness, where she hath a place prepared
of God, that they should feed her there a thousand two
hundred and threescore days. (Rev. 12:1–6)

So a great sign or portent appears in the heavens. She represents the faithful remnant of Israel, she who was to give
birth to the Christ, but who did so in travail and pain (Is.
26:17-21). We know she is Israel because of the dream
given to Joseph—"And he dreamed yet another dream,
and told it his brethren, and said, Behold, I have dreamed
a dream more; and, behold, the sun and the moon and
the eleven stars made obeisance to me" (Gen. 37:9)—Joseph himself would have been the twelfth star. And there
is clearly some sort of astrological significance to the fact
that the woman (Virgo?) has the moon under her feet, the
sun in her midriff, and a crown of stars on her head.

A second wonder appeared in the heavens. This was a
great red dragon, identified as the devil or Satan a few
verses down (v. 9). This dragon had the combined characteristics of *all* the beasts in Daniel's vision, showing how
each pagan empire was simply Satan in a new guise. This
was no less true of Satan's Roman period, during which he
sought to devour the Child Christ through the agency of
Herod the Great. The seven heads here also identifies him
with the beast of Rome that appears in the next chapter.

Apparently Satan had drawn a third of the angels into
his rebellion against God, dragging them down to earth

with him. His intent was to devour the Christ as soon as he was born, but the attempt was unsuccessful. In this passage, the narrative jumps from Christ's birth to His ascension. The fact that this child is Christ is confirmed by the fact that the child was destined to rule all the nations with a rod of iron. This was prophesied of the Messiah in the Old Testament (Ps. 2: 9), and is applied to Christ later in Revelation (Rev. 19:15), and to His shared rule with His saints earlier (Rev. 2:27). There is no reason to change the identification here.

Having given birth to the Messiah, faithful Israel fled to the wilderness where she was nourished and provided for by God for three and a half years.

THE DEATH OF ACCUSATION

> And there was war in heaven: Michael and his angels fought against the dragon; and the dragon fought and his angels, And prevailed not; neither was their place found any more in heaven. And the great dragon was cast out, that old serpent, called the Devil, and Satan, which deceiveth the whole world: he was cast out into the earth, and his angels were cast out with him. And I heard a loud voice saying in heaven, Now is come salvation, and strength, and the kingdom of our God, and the power of his Christ: for the accuser of our brethren is cast down, which accused them before our God day and night. And they overcame him by the blood of the Lamb, and by the word of their testimony; and they loved not their lives unto the death. Therefore rejoice,

ye heavens, and ye that dwell in them. Woe to the inhabiters of the earth and of the sea! for the devil is
come down unto you, having great wrath, because he
knoweth that he hath but a short time. (Rev. 12:7–12)

And there was war in Heaven. In the preceding verses, the
woman who was to give birth had to flee from the dragon
into the wilderness. I take verses 7 and following as a flash-
back, showing how that earlier circumstance had come
about. The dragon had been in the heavenly places, but
had now been thrown down. Having been thrown down,
he continued his career of malice, pursuing the woman.

The reason this happened was that Michael the archan-
gel (Jude 9) and his angels fought against the dragon (v.
7) and his angels, and as a result, there was no place re-
maining in Heaven for the dragon (v. 8). In the next verse,
the dragon is identified—the old serpent, the devil, or Satan, the deceiver of the entire world (v. 9). He was cast
down to earth, and all his angels together with him. This
plainly identifies the devil of the New Testament with the
serpent in the Garden.

Taking all of Scripture together, we learn that this "casting down" happened in the death, burial and resurrection
of Jesus. "Now is the judgment of this world: now shall the
prince of this world be cast out" (John 12:31). This is why
the next verse declares that "now is come salvation, and
strength, and the kingdom of our God, and the power of
his Christ" (v. 10). When the defender of sinners was vindicated on earth in the resurrection, the accuser of sinners
was deposed in the heavens.

The meaning of the devil being cast down is that he is no longer able to accuse the brethren *before God*, as he would do both day and night. The accusing and prosecutorial nature of the devil is seen plainly in the Old Testament (Job 1-2; Zech. 3). And this ended in the cross. "And having spoiled principalities and powers, he made a shew of them openly, triumphing over them in it" (Col. 2:15).

"Forasmuch then as the children are partakers of flesh and blood, he also himself likewise took part of the same; *that through death he might destroy him* that had the power of death, that is, the devil; And deliver them who through fear of death were all their lifetime subject to bondage" (Heb. 2:14–15).

The resurrection of Jesus was the death of accusation in the heavenly places. The accusations in the presence of God are received no longer. This does not mean that the accusations have vanished, but they have been cast down to earth. And this means—if we are paying attention to the gospel message—we should embrace on earth what has been accomplished in Heaven. That is how we pray, is it not? We want to have God's will done on earth as it has been done in Heaven.

So the faithful believers on earth have both a shield and a sword. They defend themselves, and they go out as overcomers. The shield is the blood of the Lamb (v. 11), able to withstand every accusation that an exiled devil can throw at them. Elsewhere in Scripture the shield is faith (Eph. 6:16), which means the flaming darts that the devil throws must be fiery doubts—given their heat by means of accusation. The fact that the devil has no more audience in Heaven with this kind of thing does not mean he never gains an audience here. But he can only do so by means of a lie.

The sword of the faithful believers is their word of witness and testimony, coupled with their willingness to die (v. 11). We defend ourselves from accusation by means of the blood of Christ, and we are to conquer the world by means of our testimony to the blood of Christ.

The call is given to the heavens, along with those who dwell there—rejoice that the devil is banished. There is a concurrent woe for the inhabitants of the earth and sea (v. 12). The devil has been thrown down, and is furious, and he knows he has a very short time to stamp out the infant church.

EXODUS IN THE FIRST CENTURY

> And when the dragon saw that he was cast unto the earth, he persecuted the woman which brought forth the man child. And to the woman were given two wings of a great eagle, that she might fly into the wilderness, into her place, where she is nourished for a time, and times, and half a time, from the face of the serpent. And the serpent cast out of his mouth water as a flood after the woman, that he might cause her to be carried away of the flood. And the earth helped the woman, and the earth opened her mouth, and swallowed up the flood which the dragon cast out of his mouth. And the dragon was wroth with the woman, and went to make war with the remnant of her seed, which keep the commandments of God, and have the testimony of Jesus Christ. (Rev. 12:13–17)

Remember the theme of this entire book. God is in the process of divorcing the Old Jerusalem and preparing a bride for His Son in the New Jerusalem. This passage should be understood in the context of the build up to the destruction of Jerusalem in 70 A.D.

The dragon, identified as Satan earlier, and also described in this same passage as a serpent, is furious with the woman who gave birth to the "man child." The faithful remnant of Israel had brought forth the Messiah, and when the devil was thrown down to earth, he persecuted the Judean church. They had been prepared for this by the Lord's solemn warning.

"When ye therefore shall see the abomination of desolation, spoken of by Daniel the prophet, stand in the holy place, (whoso readeth, let him understand:) Then let them which be in Judaea flee into the mountains" (Matt. 24:15–16).

When the armies of Rome come, you are to go. And this is precisely what the Judean church did—seeking refuge in Pella in 66 A.D. She is there protected for three and a half years (a time, times, and half a time). A flood of wrath comes, but the earth absorbs it—as unbelieving Jewry absorbed the wrath that missed the Christians.

All of this is Exodus imagery—the believers who escaped from the demolition of Jerusalem were spared in just the same way that the Jews were delivered from Pharaoh. "Ye have seen what I did unto the Egyptians, and how I bare you on eagles' wings, and brought you unto myself" (Ex. 19:4; cf. Dt.32:11-12). God took them out of Egypt on the wings of an eagle, and He brought these faithful Christians out of Judea on the wings of an eagle also. This also helps to identify the corrupt establishment in Jerusalem with Egypt itself. They had become the enemies of God. We saw this identification of Jerusalem with Egypt in the previous chapter, and here it continues. "And their dead bodies shall lie in the street of the great city, which spiritually is called Sodom and Egypt, where also our Lord was crucified" (Rev. 11:8).

The dragon continued in its fury. Not able to kill the woman, he turns to make war on the remainder of her offspring (in this case, it is likely we are talking about the Gentile church). These are plainly identified as believers—they keep the commandments of God, and they have the testimony of Jesus Christ.

CHAPTER 13

THE FIRST BEAST

And I stood upon the sand of the sea, and saw a beast rise up out of the sea, having seven heads and ten horns, and upon his horns ten crowns, and upon his heads the name of blasphemy. And the beast which I saw was like unto a leopard, and his feet were as the feet of a bear, and his mouth as the mouth of a lion: and the dragon gave him his power, and his seat, and great authority. And I saw one of his heads as it were wounded to death; and his deadly wound was healed: and all the world wondered after the beast. And they worshipped the dragon which gave power unto the

beast: and they worshipped the beast, saying, Who is
like unto the beast? who is able to make war with him?
(Rev. 13:1–4)

At the beginning of this next chapter, we have the introduction of the great beast from the sea. This is one area where
most commentators agree—a remarkable feat given the nature of this book. This beast is best understood as representing the Roman Empire, for some of the following reasons:

The sea represents the Gentile nations generally (Is.
17:12; 60:5). In Daniel 7:1-7, we are given a description
of four beasts, representing successive empires. The fourth
in that series was the Roman Empire, and the description
of the beast here largely matches the description given by
Daniel. At the same time, certain features of the earlier
beasts from Daniel are incorporated by John into his description of Rome, making Rome here something of a culmination beast. For example, the image of leopard, lion
and bear are used by Daniel for the earlier empires, but by
John here they are incorporated into Rome. And when in
one instance Paul was delivered from the power of Rome,
he described it as being delivered from a lion (2 Tim. 4:17).

Rome was known as the city of seven hills, and additional information gleaned later (from Rev. 17: 9-11) tells us
that the seven heads of the beast were doubly symbolic.
They represented seven kings, and they also represented
seven hills. Rome was known in the ancient world as the
city of seven hills, and just as we recognize the Big Easy
as New Orleans, or the Windy City as Chicago, so the first

century readers would have known instantly that we were talking about Rome.

The fact that the seven heads were seven kings also helps us date the book using internal evidence. Beginning with Julius Caesar, Rome had seven emperors during this period. They were Julius Caesar, Augustus, Tiberius, Caligula, Claudius, and Nero, followed by Galba who reigned a "short while," meaning just a few months. These heads, we are told, were crowned with blasphemy, and it is striking that Caesar worship began in the reign of Augustus, and was particularly intense in Asia Minor—where this book was addressed.

This also helps us understand the head wound that the beast suffered, but then recovered from miraculously. So John tells us that five emperors "were," meaning that the sixth "is." Nero was forced to commit suicide in 68 A.D. and that plunged Rome into anarchy and turmoil. It was remarkable that Rome survived at all, and it is also noteworthy that all this happened at the same time that Roman armies were besieging Jerusalem. This is internal evidence that Revelation was given during the reign of Nero, sometime before the destruction of Jerusalem.

After Nero's death, three emperors ruled within the space of one year—Galba, Otho, and Vitellius. The empire was entirely destabilized. Vespasian was the general who was fighting against Jerusalem, and so he turned things over to his son Titus, returned to Rome and restored order. The Temple of Jupiter on the Capitoline Hill was burned in 69 A.D. during the fighting. It really was a narrow go.

We should also keep in mind the fact that Satan was the spiritual authority behind Rome. It says several times in this text that the beast obtained its power from the dragon. Just as principalities and powers backed the ancient empires of the Old Testament, in the same way Satan was the spiritual force behind the throne of Rome: Satan "gave him his power, and his seat, and great authority." The scarlet color of the beast matches the dragon, not to mention the number of heads and the number of horns (Rev. 12:3; 17:3). So the beast from the sea represents the persecuting power of unbelieving political authority, embodied at that time in Rome.

This is an important anchor point for interpreting the rest of the book. If the beast from the sea is Rome, it helps us understand what some of the other symbols must be.

WAR WITH THE SAINTS

And there was given unto him a mouth speaking great things and blasphemies; and power was given unto him to continue forty and two months. And he opened his mouth in blasphemy against God, to blaspheme his name, and his tabernacle, and them that dwell in heaven. And it was given unto him to make war with the saints, and to overcome them: and power was given him over all kindreds, and tongues, and nations. And all that dwell upon the earth shall worship him, whose names are not written in the book of life of the Lamb slain from the foundation of the world. If any man have an ear, let him hear. He that leadeth into captivity shall go into captivity: he that killeth with

> the sword must be killed with the sword. Here is the
> patience and the faith of the saints. (Rev. 13:5–10)

So we are continuing to observe John's description of the beast from the sea, which is generally Rome, and specifically Nero. In this passage we have another clue that helps fix this identity. The emperors were nothing if not blasphemous. The practice of overt emperor worship had taken root during the time of Augustus, and the practice ranged from allowed to mandatory. When they took the throne, they assumed blasphemous names for themselves. *Sebastos* was one such name, and it meant "one to be worshiped." Emperors were called *dives* or *Deus*—in short, God.

The saints are being warned here that the persecution that will rain down on them will be severe—it is described as making war on them. But they are also encouraged by the fact that the severe persecution will be comparatively short. The beast was on a chain, and God was only going to let him off the chain for a mere forty-two months. We are told several times that the beast only had the power he did because it was *granted* to him. "And there was given unto him . . . and power was given unto him" (verse five). Despite the blasphemous claims, the power of the beast did not originate with him. He had it from Satan, and Satan was bounded by the will of God.

As it happened, the first Roman persecution of the church began under Nero, and it lasted for forty-two months. After the great fire in Rome, when suspicion fell on Nero for starting it, he responded by scapegoating the Christians. That persecution was fierce, and according to Tacitus, it included Christians being treated with pitch, and then set up as torches for a dinner party Nero was hosting. This persecution began in 64 A.D. and ended in 68 A.D. when Nero was forced to commit suicide—forty two months later.

The power to war against the saints was a power that included rule over all "kindreds, tongues, and nations." The inhabitants of the earth, if their names were not in the Book of Life, would give themselves to him in worship. It is striking that the Book of Life is described as belonging to the Lamb, and the Lamb is described as having been slain from the foundation of the world.

The saints are encouraged with the words Jesus was accustomed to use—if a man has ears to hear, then he should hear. They are also encouraged to endure, knowing that the God of justice sees what their persecutor is doing. There is no need for them to take up the sword in self-defense. The one who leads into captivity will be led into captivity, and the one who kills with the sword will die by the sword—just as Nero was vicious in his cruelty to others, so at the end he was forced to fall on his own sword.

This is the patience and faith of the saints. Hold on, John tells them.

THE OTHER BEAST

> And I beheld another beast coming up out of the earth; and he had two horns like a lamb, and he spake as a dragon. And he exerciseth all the power of the first beast before him, and causeth the earth and them which dwell therein to worship the first beast, whose

deadly wound was healed. And he doeth great wonders, so that he maketh fire come down from heaven
on the earth in the sight of men, And deceiveth them
that dwell on the earth by the means of those miracles
which he had power to do in the sight of the beast; saying to them that dwell on the earth, that they should
make an image to the beast, which had the wound by
a sword, and did live. And he had power to give life
unto the image of the beast, that the image of the beast
should both speak, and cause that as many as would
not worship the image of the beast should be killed.
(Rev. 13:11–15)

We have identified the beast from the sea—a great and
threatening beast—with the Roman Empire. Its seven
heads are seven hills, and its seven heads are also seven
kings—the sixth one, Nero, reigning at the time the Revelation was given.

But we now come to a lesser beast, a beast who arises from
the land. This beast does not look terrifying the same way
the sea beast does because it looks like a lamb. But it *speaks*
like a dragon, showing that it is just as evil as the sea beast,
and like the dragon Satan, who is behind the sea beast.

In order to ascertain the identity of the land beast, we have
to piece together a few clues. The first is that John identifies
this land beast with the false prophet to come later.

And I saw three unclean spirits like frogs come out of
the mouth of the dragon, and out of the mouth of the
beast, *and out of the mouth of the false prophet.* (Rev.
16:13)

And the beast was taken, *and with him the false proph-et* that wrought miracles before him, with which he deceived them that had received the mark of the beast, and them that worshipped his image. These both were cast alive into a lake of fire burning with brimstone. (Rev. 19:20)

And the devil that deceived them was cast into the lake of fire and brimstone, where the beast *and the false prophet* are, and shall be tormented day and night for ever and ever. (Rev. 20:10)

So the land beast is described as a religious figure (a prophet), but one who gives a blessing to those who would worship the sea beast, Rome. There is obviously a cozy relationship with Rome. This beast also has the power of working signs and wonders. This beast comes up out of the earth—the word for this is *ge*, which should be best under-stood here as the *land*, meaning the land of Israel. Putting all this together, I take the land beast as representing the priesthood of apostate Israel, with the high priest as a like-ly representative.

We have an example of this in how the religious leaders of the Jews treated Jesus.

Then gathered the chief priests and the Pharisees a council, and said, What do we? for this man doeth many miracles. If we let him thus alone, all men will believe on him: and the Romans shall come and take away both our place and nation. (John 11:47–48)

> And Caiaphas, being high priest that year, spoke for them all when he said that Jesus must die for the nation. (John 11:49)

But what about the signs and sorcery? We have indications of that kind of behavior among the Jews also.

> But there was a certain man, called Simon, which beforetime in the same city used sorcery, and bewitched the people of Samaria, giving out that himself was some great one. (Acts 8:9)

> And when they had gone through the isle unto Paphos, they found a certain sorcerer, a false prophet, a Jew, whose name was Bar-jesus. (Acts 13:6)

Some of them even tried to use the name of Jesus as though it were a charm.

> Then certain of the vagabond Jews, exorcists, took upon them to call over them which had evil spirits the name of the Lord Jesus, saying, We adjure you by Jesus whom Paul preacheth. (Acts 19:13)

The Jewish rebels who finally brought about the destruction of Jerusalem were a very different group from the Jewish quislings who worked hand in glove together with Rome. Satan was behind Rome, and these men were prostrate before Rome, making them a synagogue of Satan. They were, as Jesus once put it, of their father the devil (John 8:44). The Jewish leadership at this time was demonic.

NERON KAISAR

> And he causeth all, both small and great, rich and
> poor, free and bond, to receive a mark in their right
> hand, or in their foreheads: And that no man might
> buy or sell, save he that had the mark, or the name of
> the beast, or the number of his name. Here is wisdom.
> Let him that hath understanding count the number of
> the beast: for it is the number of a man; and his num-
> ber is Six hundred threescore and six. (Rev. 13:16–18)

In order to understand this (often misconstrued) section
of Revelation, we must (literally) return to our ABCs. In
English, we use *Roman* letters and *Arabic* numerals. When
we want to spell a number out, we write *three*. When we
want to use a symbol for it, we write 3. We are so used to
this system that we hardly even reflect on it. It is a very
good system, if I may say so.

But Hebrew, Greek and Latin did not work this way.
They did not use Arabic symbols for their numbers, but
rather used the letters of their own alphabets for both pho-
netic sounds and for numbers. Thus, in Greek, the first
letter *alpha* (corresponding to our letter *a*) made its particular vowel sound, but it also represented the numerical
value of one. I trust you are all still with me. This system
was common in the ancient world, and is called *gematria*.

If English had an analogous system, it would be easy to
compute the numerical value of our names. For example,
my name is Douglas. All we would have to do is add the
value of the numbers up: D (4), O (60), U (300), G (7), L

(30), A (1), and S (100). The number of my name would therefore be 502. And while this strikes us as odd and contrived (because we don't do it), it was very common in the ancient world. Graffiti at Pompeii has been found that said, "I love her whose number is 545."[2] There are not enough digits there for it to be her phone number. And the Roman historian Seutonius pointed out (about Nero) that some doggerel poetry was circulating in Rome that pointed out the numerical value of "Nero," and "murdered his mother" were the same. This was pertinent because Nero *had* murdered his mother. And because we are talking about a particular intellectual skill set, someone once figured out that if you rearrange the letters of *Presbyterians* you can spell out Britney Spears. There are always people like this, and so we can be grateful that gematria died out before Facebook was invented.

Now mark this. John knew the name of the person *he* was thinking of, and he also believed that any reasonably clever member of the churches in Asia would be able to figure it out also. Let the one "with understanding" calculate the identity of the beast. It would be odd in the extreme if young Demetrius of Ephesus stayed up late the night after Revelation was read to their church, and in the morning asked his father who Henry Kissinger might be.

The system John was inviting them to use would have been obvious to them all. But it couldn't have been *too*

---

2. Adolf Deissmann, *Light from the Ancient East Illustrated by Recently Discovered Texts of the Graeco-Roman World* (1927; repr., Grand Rapids: Eerdmans, 1980), 276. Cited in Eckhard Schnabel, *40 Questions about the End Times* (Grand Rapids: Kregel Publications, 2011), 186.

obvious, or else the officials censoring the mail leaving Patmos would have found out that John was writing seditious letters to his churches. The land beast that represented Rome is destroyed in this book. And so John was inviting the readers to transliterate the Greek name *Nero Caesar* into Hebrew, which the censors would not pick up on. In Hebrew, it would have been *Nrwn Qsr*. Once the vowel markings were added, as commentator Larry Ball points out, it would have been pronounced as *Neron Kaiser*.[3]

So what is the numerical value of *Nrwn Qsr?* As it happens, it is $50 + 200 + 6 + 50 + 100 + 60 + 200 = 666$. Nero was the head of the beast who was ruling at the time this revelation was given, and it seems to me that his identity as the sixth head of the seven-headed beast is secure.

It is worth mentioning that in the original, there is nothing like 666 or six six six. The value is found in the sum, in the *total*. The number given is six hundred and sixty six.

One additional comment should be made about the mark of the beast. The persecution included shutting believers off from the means of sustaining life, using economic choke points. You were not allowed to buy or sell unless you were willing to take the mark, or the name, or the number of the name onto your right hand or forehead. This is a diabolical parody of God's requirement for faithful Jews, who were to bind the law of God on their *hand* and on their *forehead*.

3. Larry Ball, *Blessed Is He Who Reads* (Fountain Inn, SC: Victorious Hope Publishing, 2015), 150-154.

CHAPTER 14

144,000 SAINTS

And I looked, and, lo, a Lamb stood on the mount Sion, and with him an hundred forty and four thousand, having his Father's name written in their foreheads. And I heard a voice from heaven, as the voice of many waters, and as the voice of a great thunder: and I heard the voice of harpers harping with their harps: And they sung as it were a new song before the throne, and before the four beasts, and the elders: and no man could learn that song but the hundred and forty and four thousand, which were redeemed from the earth. These are they which were not defiled with women;

for they are virgins. These are they which follow the Lamb whithersoever he goeth. These were redeemed from among men, being the firstfruits unto God and to the Lamb. And in their mouth was found no guile: for they are without fault before the throne of God. (Rev. 14:1–5)

As we come to the fourteenth chapter of Revelation, we do so having been introduced to an evil travesty of the Trinity—the great dragon (Satan), the sea beast (which was Rome), and the land beast (which represented the priestly leadership in Jerusalem). As this chapter opens, the contrast couldn't be sharper than it is. Those enslaved to the beast in the previous chapter had the mark of the beast on their right hand, or on their forehead. Here the 144,000 have the name of the Father on *their* foreheads. Everyone has the name of someone on their forehead.

The scene here appears to be in the heavens, and not on earth. We saw in chapter seven that the 144,000 likely represented the total number of the elect, which means they were not assembled on the *earthly* Mt. Zion in Jerusalem. Rather, the scene is the heavenly Jerusalem, the New Jerusalem that descends from Heaven at the conclusion of Revelation. In Hebrews 12:22, it teaches us that in worship, the saints of God assemble in a heavenly Jerusalem, and it mentions Mt. Zion expressly. The harpers here are described as being "before the throne," and the 144,000 are said to have been redeemed "from the earth." All this places the scene in Heaven.

So we have here a wonderful image of the perseverance and preservation of the saints. In chapter seven, the
144,000 were still on earth, and they were all sealed to
protect them there. Here in Heaven their number is un-
diminished—not one was lost. The reason is plain. These
were the only ones who could learn the "new song" that the
harpers were playing. These men were virgins, undefiled
with woman. This is talking about spiritual fornication, or
idolatry. It is not talking about lawful marital relations,
which are not defiling at all (Heb. 13:4). These are called
virgins because together they all constitute the Virgin who
descends out of Heaven like an undefiled bride at the end
of this book (Rev. 19:7). They are called virgins because
they have nothing to do with the great harlot, who is to be
introduced shortly. In 2 Cor. 11:2, Paul uses virginity as
a symbol of spiritual integrity. Moreover, these are those
who "follow the Lamb whithersoever he goeth." They are
described as being without fault before the throne of God.

A close examination of this passage and the description
of heavenly worship in Hebrews 12:18-23 is likely to be
rewarding. Both scenes take place on Mt. Zion. In Revelation the worshipers are the firstfruits and in Hebrews they
are described as being the church of the first born. And
the 144,000 represent the entire number of the elect, as
do the worshipers in Hebrews, whose names are "written
in heaven."

THE GOSPEL HAS BEEN PREACHED

> And I saw another angel fly in the midst of heaven,
> having the everlasting gospel to preach unto them that
> dwell on the earth, and to every nation, and kindred,
> and tongue, and people, Saying with a loud voice, Fear
> God, and give glory to him; for the hour of his judg-
> ment is come: and worship him that made heaven, and
> earth, and the sea, and the fountains of waters. (Rev.
> 14:6–7)

We should first consider the fact that in this place the gospel is being proclaimed by a flying angel in the midst of
the sky. We know from the record of Scripture that the
gospel was fundamentally entrusted to the *church*, and not
to angels (Matt. 28:18-20). But the fact that men are the
ordinary preachers of gospel does not require the angels to
be silent about it, as in this instance the angel isn't. When
Paul chides the Galatians for drifting away from the gospel, he says this: "But though we, or an angel from heaven,
preach any other gospel unto you than that which we have
preached unto you, let him be accursed" (Gal. 1:8). The
problem here was that it was a different gospel, and not
the fact that it was preached by an angel. So ordinarily
men are to preach the gospel, but this proclamation from
the heavens fits in with what we are taught elsewhere.

We are coming to the climax of God's wrath being poured
out over Jerusalem, and Jesus had predicted this very thing
before that destruction. "And this gospel of the kingdom
shall be preached in all the world for a witness unto all

nations; and then shall the end come" (Matt. 24:14). This angel speaks to all nations—to "them that dwell on the earth, and to every nation, and kindred, and tongue, and people." This is a sign that the demolition of Jerusalem is about to happen.

This angel preaches, it says, with a "loud voice." What is the content of what he says? What is the shape of this everlasting gospel? What the angel says here fits in with what we are taught elsewhere. He says that men are to "fear God" (Luke 1:50; Luke 12:5). "But in every nation he that feareth him, and worketh righteousness, is accepted with him" (Acts 10:35). He says that men must "give glory to him" (Matt. 5:16; Matt. 9:8). "Insomuch that the multitude wondered, when they saw the dumb to speak, the maimed to be whole, the lame to walk, and the blind to see: and they glorified the God of Israel" (Matt. 15:31). He says that "the hour of his judgment is come" (John 12:23, 31-32). "And when he is come, he will reprove the world of sin, and of righteousness, and of judgment: Of sin, because they believe not on me; Of righteousness, because I go to my Father, and ye see me no more; Of judgment, because the prince of this world is judged" (John 16:8–11). And as we saw in the first chapters of Genesis, the God of the gospel is the God who made all things—whether "heaven, and earth, and the sea," or "the fountains of waters."

In short, what the angel declared in the preparation for Jerusalem's destruction sounds very much like what the apostle Paul declared.

God that made the world and all things therein, seeing that he is Lord of heaven and earth, dwelleth not in temples made with hands; Neither is worshipped with men's hands, as though he needed any thing, seeing he giveth to all life, and breath, and all things; And hath made of one blood all nations of men for to dwell on all the face of the earth, and hath determined the times before appointed, and the bounds of their habitation; That they should seek the Lord, if haply they might feel after him, and find him, though he be not far from every one of us: For in him we live, and move, and have our being; as certain also of your own poets have said, For we are also his offspring. Forasmuch then as we are the offspring of God, we ought not to think that the Godhead is like unto gold, or silver, or stone, graven by art and man's device. And the times of this ignorance God winked at; but now commandeth all men every where to repent: Because he hath appointed a day, in the which he will judge the world in righteousness by that man whom he hath ordained; whereof he hath given assurance unto all men, in that he hath raised him from the dead. (Acts 17:24–31)

JERUSALEM, THE HARLOT

And there followed another angel, saying, Babylon is fallen, is fallen, that great city, because she made all nations drink of the wine of the wrath of her fornication. (Rev. 14:8)

This is the first place in the Revelation where the *name* Babylon makes its entrance. The Babylon that is introduced in this place has her fall actually described a few chapters later, in chapter eighteen. A great deal of ink has been spilled in trying to identify this Babylon, and both here and in the sections that follow I will hazard my reasons for supposing Babylon to be Jerusalem—the city doomed to destruction throughout the course of this entire book.

We have already encountered the dragon, who is Satan, the beast from the sea, who is Rome, and the land beast, who is the corrupt leadership of the Jews. My understanding of this is that the image of the great harlot, the wanton Babylon, is this third group under a different image. The corruptocrats ruling in Jerusalem had a cozy relationship with Rome that they did not want threatened (Jn. 11:48), and we are told in the description that follows that the woman rides on the back of the seven-headed beast, who is Rome. The establishment in Jerusalem was dependent upon Rome.

If we look at both the parallels and contrasts here, the picture comes into focus. The entire book is about the rivalry of two women, pictured for us in Scripture in two different ways. In Galatians, they are Hagar and Sarah (Gal. 4:24). In this place they are the unfaithful wife, given over to harlotry, and the faithful and virginal bride, adorned for her husband. They are both described as Jerusalem, they are both described under the image of the holy city—but one of them is in fact an unholy city.

Hear ye this, O house of Jacob, Which are called by the name of Israel, And are come forth out of the waters of Judah, Which swear by the name of the LORD, And make mention of the God of Israel, *but not in truth*, nor in righteousness. *For they call themselves of the holy city*, and stay themselves upon the God of Israel; The LORD of hosts is his name. (Is. 48:1–2)

But another image is given to us by the prophet Isaiah as well.

Awake, awake; put on thy strength, O Zion; Put on thy beautiful garments, *O Jerusalem, the holy city*: For henceforth there shall no more come into thee the un-circumcised and the unclean. (Is. 52:1)

The nation of Israel was supposed to be a testimony to the nations, but they had missed their calling. Instead of serving as a called nation, showing all the nations how God dealt with men, they took their chosen status as meaning what God had said it did not mean. God had not chosen them because they were so wonderful. *"The LORD did not set his love upon you, nor choose you, because ye were more in number than any people; for ye were the fewest of all people"* (Deut. 7:7).

Instead of revealing God's goodness to the nations, Israel had fallen away and become a great harlot. She "made all nations drink of the wine of the wrath of her fornication." The great court outside the Temple sanctuary was called the Court of the Gentiles, and it was reserved for them to worship God. But the corrupt oligarchy in Jerusalem had filled that court up with sacrificial animals which represented the Jews, and squeezed out the Gentiles. Jesus mentions this as He cleansed the Temple. "And he taught, saying unto them, Is it not written, My house shall be called *of all nations* the house of prayer? but ye have made it a den of thieves" (Mark 11:17).

Jerusalem was a great city, but this just contributed to the greatness of her fall.

UNDILUTED TORMENT

> And the third angel followed them, saying with a loud voice, If any man worship the beast and his image, and receive his mark in his forehead, or in his hand, The same shall drink of the wine of the wrath of God, which is poured out without mixture into the cup of his indignation; and he shall be tormented with fire and brimstone in the presence of the holy angels, and in the presence of the Lamb: And the smoke of their torment ascendeth up for ever and ever: and they have no rest day nor night, who worship the beast and his image, and whosoever receiveth the mark of his name. Here is the patience of the saints: here are they that keep the commandments of God, and the faith of Jesus. (Rev. 14:9–12)

A third angel arrives and delivers his warning in a loud voice. This warning concerns anyone who worships the beast and/or the image of the beast. This would be done by receiving the mark of the beast on the forehead or on the hand. Taking such a mark is an indication of total dedication, total allegiance. That being the case, God's response to this impudence is total judgment.

We saw earlier that those who refused this mark were denied the privilege of buying and selling (Rev. 13:17). But those who take the mark are given the wine of the wrath of God to drink. It is the wine of wrath (*thymos*), and it is poured into the cup of wrath (*orge*), and it is poured in an unmixed form into the cup they must drink from. In this life, the wrath of God is revealed against the ungodliness of men (Rom. 1:18), but in this life it is always *mixed* with common grace. The ancients used to dilute wine with water in order to "cut" it, and they also used to add spices to their wine in order to increase the kick. The two words used here refer to both practices, one in reverse. This wine is *mingled* with spices and *unmixed* with water. It is a *hard* drink.

What is the drink? It is to be tormented with fire and brimstone, in the presence of the holy angels and in the presence of the Lamb. They suffer their torments with Jesus watching—which should be enough to make us reject the saccharine portraits of Jesus that some love to paint. This is a terrifying picture—it is the wrath of the *Lamb*. It is better to have mountains fall on you and crush you than to have to deal with the wrath of the Lamb (Rev. 6:16). Fire and brimstone destroyed Sodom and Gomorrah (Gen. 19:24). God promises to do this to the wicked generally. "Upon the wicked he shall rain snares, fire and brimstone, and a horrible tempest: *this shall be the portion of their cup*" (Ps. 11:6). And this is the composition of the final lake of fire—it is a lake of fire and brimstone (Rev. 20:10). Brimstone is an archaic word for sulfur.

They have no rest, day or night. The smoke of their torment ascends forever. In this they are like their forerunner in judgment. "Even as Sodom and Gomorrha, and the cities about them . . . are set forth for an example, suffering the vengeance of eternal fire" (Jude 7). These cities, totally wrecked and gone, are still described as suffering the vengeance of *eternal fire*. The destruction of Edom is described by Isaiah in a very similar way.

"It shall not be quenched night nor day; The smoke thereof shall go up for ever: From generation to generation it shall lie waste; None shall pass through it for ever and ever" (Is. 34:10).

This description of ultimate judgment is either literal or symbolic. If it is literal, then it is really bad. If it is symbolic (as the echoes of Edom and Sodom seem to indicate), then the reality is worse. Symbols are always less than the reality they represent.

Considering their final destination, those who keep the commandments of God, and those who keep the faith of Jesus, are exhibiting the peculiar patience of the saints. They can withstand the torments that men deliver because they have no intention of risking the torments that will happen in the presence of the Lamb.

JERUSALEM, GOD'S WINEPRESS

> And I heard a voice from heaven saying unto me, Write, Blessed are the dead which die in the Lord from henceforth: Yea, saith the Spirit, that they may rest from their labours; and their works do follow them.

And I looked, and behold a white cloud, and upon the
cloud one sat like unto the Son of man, having on his
head a golden crown, and in his hand a sharp sickle.
And another angel came out of the temple, crying with
a loud voice to him that sat on the cloud, Thrust in thy
sickle, and reap: for the time is come for thee to reap;
for the harvest of the earth is ripe. And he that sat
on the cloud thrust in his sickle on the earth; and the
earth was reaped. And another angel came out of the
temple which is in heaven, he also having a sharp sickle. And another angel came out from the altar, which
had power over fire; and cried with a loud cry to him
that had the sharp sickle, saying, Thrust in thy sharp
sickle, and gather the clusters of the vine of the earth;
for her grapes are fully ripe. And the angel thrust in
his sickle into the earth, and gathered the vine of the
earth, and cast it into the great winepress of the wrath
of God. And the winepress was trodden without the
city, and blood came out of the winepress, even unto
the horse bridles, by the space of a thousand and six
hundred furlongs. (Rev. 14:13-20)

The martyrs earlier had been gathered under the altar
(Rev. 6:9), and their prayers were on the golden altar
(Rev. 8:3). They were blessed, but not exactly at rest—
they were given white robes so they could rest "for a little
season." They cried out in a loud voice for God to show
His righteous vengeance. But now the times of vengeance
have come, the time was complete. Jerusalem was now to
be destroyed, and this means that all the saints who die

from this point on are blessed. There are seven benedictions pronounced in Revelation, and this is the second of the seven (Rev. 1:3; 14:13; 16:15; 19:9; 20:6; 22:7, 14). The saints who will die from this point on have the privilege of resting from their labors (v. 13), and their works follow them to their rest. A voice from Heaven declared this benediction, and the Spirit reinforced it.

A few verses earlier in this chapter, we saw the cup of the wine of God's wrath, which the ungodly had to drink down. Here we see how that wine was to be made, and in a macabre twist we see that those who have to drink the wine are themselves the crushed grapes that make up the wine. The stage is set when John sees the Lord Jesus, one "like a son of Man" (Dan. 7:13). He is seated on a white cloud, just as the one like a son of Man comes on the clouds of heaven in Daniel. He wears a golden crown and holds a sharp sickle in His hand. The one on the cloud wields His sickle and the earth is reaped, and then right after this, an angel with a sharp sickle does the same thing. While some commentators take this as two harvests, I take this double image as indicating that the authority for the final reaping comes from Christ, but the mission is actually accomplished by an angelic executive. Some might wonder that an angel tells Christ to wield His sickle, but the angel is simply a messenger, and he comes out of the Temple as a herald of God.

And so an angel comes out of the Temple, and calls to the Lord to harvest the earth, which He does. When His angelic executive with the sickle comes out of the Temple with *his* sickle, yet another angel comes from the altar (where the martyrs were) and tells him to reap the grapes,

grapes that were fully ripe. These were the "clusters of the vine of the earth," about to become the vintage of 70 A.D.

This was a harvest of great wrath, taking the grapes of wrath, using the sickle of wrath, and resulting in the grapes being thrown into the winepress of wrath. The wine of wrath was made from the ungodly, crushing them, and thereby treading out the wine that the ungodly had to drink. They had to drink the dregs of their own damnation.

Although the earlier description of wrath sounded global, with the Son of Man putting His sickle to the *earth* (Rev. 14:16), and the executive angel doing it to the *earth* as well (Rev. 14:18), we see from the context that this catastrophic judgment is actually a local one, even though horrific. This winepress of the wrath of God was located "without the city," clearly Jerusalem. The word rendered as earth in the preceding verses is *ge*, which should better be rendered as *land* in this context. This wine press of wrath was set up in the land of Judea, outside the doomed city of Jerusalem.

And when the judgment commenced, blood came out of the winepress—human blood—and it ran as a river for 1600 furlongs, as deep as a horse's bridle. A question remains whether this is to be understood as a literal river of blood. Initially that seems extremely unlikely—the human body holds about six quarts of blood, and 1600 furlongs is about 200 miles. The river would be about four feet deep (up to a horse's bridle), and then we would have to estimate the (considerable) width of the river. We are talking about millions upon millions of people. Since the number 40 is a number of judgment in the Bible, and 1600 is 40 squared, what we appear to have is the wrath of God multiplied by itself. And the imagery is not something that was formed by John's lurid imagination—it comes straight from Scripture.

> Who is this that cometh from Edom, With dyed garments from Bozrah? This that is glorious in his apparel, Travelling in the greatness of his strength? I that speak in righteousness, mighty to save. Wherefore art thou red in thine apparel, And thy garments like him that treadeth in the winefat? I have trodden the winepress alone; And of the people there was none with me: For I will tread them in mine anger, And trample them in my fury; And their blood shall be sprinkled upon my garments, And I will stain all my raiment. For the day of vengeance is in mine heart, And the year of my redeemed is come. And I looked, and there was none to help; And I wondered that there was none to uphold: Therefore mine own arm brought salvation unto me; And my fury, it upheld me. And I will tread down the people in mine anger, And make them drunk in my fury, And I will bring down their strength to the earth. (Isaiah 63:1–6)

CHAPTER 15

THE CHURCH'S VICTORY SONG

And I saw another sign in heaven, great and marvellous, seven angels having the seven last plagues; for in them is filled up the wrath of God. And I saw as it were a sea of glass mingled with fire: and them that had gotten the victory over the beast, and over his image, and over his mark, and over the number of his name, stand on the sea of glass, having the harps of God. And they sing the song of Moses the servant of God, and the song of the Lamb, saying, Great and marvellous are thy works, Lord God Almighty; just and true are thy ways, thou King of saints. Who shall not fear thee,

O Lord, and glorify thy name? for thou only art holy:
for all nations shall come and worship before thee; for
thy judgments are made manifest. (Rev. 15:1–4)

Seven angels are introduced here, and we are given sort of
a prelude to the next round of judgments. Their approach
is said to be another "sign in heaven," and it was a sign that
was "great and marvelous." These are described as the sev-
en *last* plagues, meaning that we are now talking about the
final and complete destruction of Jerusalem in 70 A.D. They
bring with them the fullness of the wrath of God. This is it.

We will see in v. 6 that these angels come out of the
heavenly temple, and so it is not surprising that we also see
various aspects of temple worship described, which would
include the crystal or glass sea. This is not a lake or an
ocean out in front of the temple, but is rather the *laver* that
in the Old Testament was made of bronze, in which the
priests would wash themselves. The word here is *thalassa*, which is the same word used in the Septuagint for the
bronze laver (1 Kings 7:23). As the laver was used for purification of the worshipers, the fact that the glass here was
mingled with fire probably indicates cleansing in Heaven,
as opposed to mass destruction on earth. The original laver
for the tabernacle was small, in which the priests would
wash their hands and feet (Ex. 30:17-21; 40:30-32). Solomon's version was huge, resting on the backs of bulls. It
probably represented the Red Sea, and the great victory
that God had won for Israel there. The heavenly version
was greater still, and represented a greater victory still.

Those who had gained the victory over the beast, and over his image, and over his mark, and over the number of his name—meaning the believers who had stood firm in the Neronian persecution—were given the harps of God and they all stood on the sea of glass in order to be able to sing. They were purified at the laver, and then presented their praise.

We are told that these faithful ones sang two songs. The first was the Song of Moses, indicating that Jerusalem was identified with the old Egypt that had fallen under judgment. Just as Egypt had been left a smoldering ruin, so also Jerusalem was going to be left the same way. The second song was the Song of the Lamb, and we are given the content of that song.

This chapter began with the sign in Heaven being described as "great and marvelous," and here that phrase is repeated. They sang that the works of the Lord God Almighty were great and marvelous. He is the King of saints, and His ways are just and true. His name shall be glorified, and they sing that no one will fail to fear Him. And why? Because He alone is the Holy One, and all nations will come and worship before Him. They will do so because His judgments, in all their severity, will be made manifest now.

Just as Miriam and the women with her danced on the shores of the Red Sea, so the faithful ones who stood against Nero will sing as they stand on the Crystal Sea. The thing they share in common is the fact that they know that the songs of the saints in Heaven provide the soundtrack for judgments on earth. The ferocity of God's judgments when they finally fall upon the insolence of rebellious man is not "a problem" to be apologized for. The ferocity of God's judgments are here celebrated, and we see that they are the basis for all the nations of men coming to their senses and streaming to the Lord of the nations, the Lord Jesus Christ.

Why will the nations come and worship? Because the wrath of God has been made *manifest*.

NO MORE INTERCESSION

> And after that I looked, and, behold, the temple of the tabernacle of the testimony in heaven was opened: And the seven angels came out of the temple, having the seven plagues, clothed in pure and white linen, and having their breasts girded with golden girdles. And one of the four beasts gave unto the seven angels seven golden vials full of the wrath of God, who liveth for ever and ever. And the temple was filled with smoke from the glory of God, and from his power; and no man was able to enter into the temple, till the seven plagues of the seven angels were fulfilled. (Rev. 15:5–8)

The final moments of Jerusalem are upon her. John looked, and the sanctuary was opened, and judgment came out of her. That sanctuary is described in quite an interesting way—the "temple of the tabernacle of the testimony in heaven." The word for temple may refer to the inner sanctum, the holy of holies, which the tabernacle in the wilderness had, just as Solomon's temple did. Putting it all together, the angels came out of the holy of holies in the heavenly tabernacle. They came out of the holy of holies, where the *testimony* was kept. The ark of the covenant, capped with the mercy seat, was called the ark of the testimony (Ex. 25:22). When merciless judgment comes to you from the place of the mercy seat, you know that things are pretty bad.

The angels emerged, bringing the seven plagues with them. They were dressed in pure white linen with golden sashes wrapped around their chests. Although they came with the seven plagues, one of the four living creatures gave them seven bowls, filled up with the wrath of God. The wrath belongs to the God who lives forever and ever. The word translated *vial* in the AV is better rendered as *bowl*, and appears to match with the earlier bowls filled with incense, that is, the prayers of the saints (Rev. 5:8). Combine this with the prayers that the saints under the altar offered up (Rev. 6:9), and you can see the convergence of answered prayer and the wrath of God. Earlier they had asked, *how long?* And now that the bowls are handed out to the angels, God's answer to their question is *now*.

The glory of God, and the power of God, were manifested in the temple in the form of smoke. This is what had happened at the dedication of the tabernacle in the wilderness (Ex. 40:34-35), and at the dedication of Solomon's temple (1 Kings 8:10-11). In this instance, with no one able to enter the heavenly temple because of the smoke, it appears to be a symbolic way of saying that intercession for Jerusalem is no longer a possibility. The judgment is going to fall, and fall heavily now.

CHAPTER 16

THE FIRST BOWL: PUNISHMENT FOR IDOLATRY

> And I heard a great voice out of the temple saying to
> the seven angels, Go your ways, and pour out the vials
> of the wrath of God upon the earth. And the first went,
> and poured out his vial upon the earth; and there fell
> a noisome and grievous sore upon the men which had
> the mark of the beast, and upon them which wor-
> shipped his image. (Rev. 16:1–2)

No one could go into the heavenly Temple until after all
seven bowls were poured out (Rev. 15:8), and so that must
mean that the great voice coming out of the Temple here is

the voice of God Himself. The fact that He gives all seven angels their marching orders all at once would seem to indicate that these bowls of judgment are poured out in quick order, in rapid succession.

The effects of these seven emptied bowls run parallel to the effects of the seven trumpets blown earlier. But while the seven trumpets tended to partial destructions measured in thirds, the impact of the bowls is more complete and total. We have arrived at the crescendo, and Jerusalem is about to be no more.

In addition, we see that there are similarities with the plagues that had destroyed Egypt at the time of the Exodus (Ex. 9:8-12), and the meaning of this appears to be that the old Jerusalem has become her ancient adversary Egypt, and that the hated Christians were about to be delivered through a new Exodus, and were to take their place as the new Israel.

Those Jews who had the mark of the beast—who had cried that they had no king but Caesar—were afflicted with grievous sores. They prided themselves on being free from idolatry, but they were in fact in bondage to idolatry. These sores appeared on those who "worshiped his image." This particular plague in response to covenantal infidelity had been promised to Israel centuries before, and in a way that linked them with Egypt.

> The LORD will smite thee *with the botch of Egypt*, and with the emerods, and with the scab, and with the itch, whereof thou canst not be healed . . . The LORD shall smite thee in the knees, and in the legs, with a sore

botch that cannot be healed, from the sole of thy foot
unto the top of thy head. (Deut. 28:27, 35)

Deuteronomy says that they are sores that cannot be
healed, and that would appear to be the case here. The
sores appear at the first bowl of wrath, but those afflicted
with them are still suffering from them when the fifth bowl
is poured out (v. 11).

THE SECOND BOWL: JUDGMENT AT THE SEA

And the second angel poured out his vial upon the sea;
and it became as the blood of a dead man: and every
living soul died in the sea. (Rev. 16:3)

As numerous commentators have pointed out, the second
bowl of wrath is similar to the judgment that was delivered
through the second trumpet. The difference has to do with
the extent of the judgment. With the trumpet judgment,
when the great mountain was pitched into the sea, a third
of the sea became blood (Rev. 8:8). The judgment was partial. Here the judgment is complete. Not only did the sea
in its entirety become blood, but it was like the blood of a
dead man—putrefying, coagulated, and clotted.

This is still the final horror falling upon the Jews in revolt, and it is reminiscent of the plague that helped destroy Egypt—with Judea now being the new Egypt. In the
first plague to afflict Egypt, the Nile turned to blood (Ex.
7:17-21).

A part of the fulfillment of this prediction by John may
have happened at the Sea of Galilee, where Josephus

recalls one encounter. Remember that this Sea was where Jesus often taught, and where many of His disciples had made their living.

> They were killed by the darts on the lake; and the Romans leaped out of their vessels, and destroyed a great many more upon the land: one might then *see the lake all bloody,* and full of dead bodies, for not one of them escaped. And a terrible stink, and a very sad sight there was on the following days over that country; for as for the shores, they were full of shipwrecks, and of *dead bodies all swelled*; and as the dead bodies were inflamed by the sun, *and putrefied*, they corrupted the air . . . (*Wars*, III.10.9, emphasis mine).

THIRD BOWL: FOR THE BLOOD OF THE PROPHETS AND MARTYRS

> And the third angel poured out his vial upon the rivers and fountains of waters; and they became blood. And I heard the angel of the waters say, Thou art righteous, O Lord, which art, and wast, and shalt be, because thou hast judged thus. For they have shed the blood of saints and prophets, and thou hast given them blood to drink; for they are worthy. And I heard another out of the altar say, Even so, Lord God Almighty, true and righteous are thy judgments. (Rev. 16:4–7)

Now comes the time for the third bowl of wrath to be poured out upon Jerusalem. The previous judgment was upon the ocean; with this plague the sentence falls upon the fresh water. Again, with the trumpet judgments, the affliction was partial. Now comes the end, when the sentence is final.

So in this segment, the third angel empties his bowl of wrath. Far from objecting, another angel, the angel of the waters, declares that the judgment is righteous. The Lord is righteous, and He is the one who was, is, and is to be. *He* is the one who has determined this calamity. The next statement by the angel of the waters helps to confirm the place where this sentence must fall. As a city, the murder of prophets was characteristically Jerusalem's signature item (2 Chron. 36:15-16; Luke 13:33-34; Acts 7:52). When it came to prophets and saints, this was a bloodthirsty city, and so it was fitting that God turned all their fresh water to blood.

Jerusalem richly deserved to have this happen to them. Jesus had predicted this would happen, and He said that the murder of prophets over generations is *why* it would happen.

> Wherefore ye be witnesses unto yourselves, that ye are the children of them which killed the prophets. Fill ye up then the measure of your fathers. Ye serpents, ye generation of vipers, how can ye escape the damnation of hell? Wherefore, behold, I send unto you prophets, and wise men, and scribes: and some of them ye shall kill and crucify; and some of them shall ye scourge in your synagogues, and persecute them from city to city: That upon you may come all the righteous blood shed upon the earth, from the blood of righteous Abel unto the blood of Zacharias son of Barachias, whom ye slew between the temple and the altar. Verily I say unto

you, All these things shall come upon this generation.
(Matt. 23:31–36)

Earlier the martyrs had cried out from under the altar,
seeking God's vengeance on their behalf (Rev. 6:9). The
tribulation of the trumpets began to answer their cry for
justice, and now the finalization of justice is imminent.
And so it is that another voice comes from the altar, echo-
ing the sentiments of the angel of the waters. *Even so, Lord
God Almighty, true and righteous are thy judgments.*

FOURTH BOWL: COVENANT SUNDOWN

And the fourth angel poured out his vial upon the
sun; and power was given unto him to scorch men
with fire. And men were scorched with great heat,
and blasphemed the name of God, which hath power
over these plagues: and they repented not to give him
glory. (Rev. 16:8–9)

As we have already seen, the judgments of these bowls are
amplified versions of the trumpet judgments. The fourth
trumpet had caused the sun to dim, along with the moon
and stars.

And the fourth angel sounded, and the third part of
the sun was smitten, and the third part of the moon,
and the third part of the stars; so as the third part of
them was darkened, and the day shone not for a third
part of it, and the night likewise. (Rev. 8:12)

But now, with the judgment of the fourth bowl, the heat of the sun was ramped up such that men were scorched by it. In the historical documents of the Jewish War, we don't have any records of extraordinary heat from the sun, and so our attention turns to a possible symbolic interpretation. This judgment is a covenant judgment, falling upon Jerusalem and Israel, just as the curses of Deuteronomy had predicted.

> The LORD will strike you with wasting disease and with fever, inflammation *and fiery heat,* and with drought and with blight and with mildew. They shall pursue you until you perish. (Deut. 28:22, ESV, emphasis added)

The striking thing about this judgment is that as this harbinger of Hell was approaching, the men under judgment did not consider repentance. Rather, they blasphemed the name of God, and they did not repent in such a way as to give Him glory. The fact that this is mentioned indicates what the appropriate response to such a judgment should have been.

FIFTH BOWL: JUDGMENT ON ROME

> And the fifth angel poured out his vial upon the seat of the beast; and his kingdom was full of darkness; and they gnawed their tongues for pain, and blasphemed the God of heaven because of their pains and their sores, and repented not of their deeds. (Rev. 16:10–11)

The way we are interpreting all these portents, the bulk of them are falling on Jerusalem. Jerusalem is the city devoted to utter destruction. But that does not mean that Rome was left unscathed. The center of attention is always Jerusalem, but the pagan nations are not out of view. Earlier in Revelation we read this: "Because thou hast kept the word of my patience, I also will keep thee from the hour of temptation, *which shall come upon all the world*, to try them that dwell upon the earth [*land*]" (Rev. 3:10). Jerusalem is ground zero, but the rest of the Roman world was not unaffected.

So when the fifth angel pours out his bowl of wrath, he pours it out on the throne of the beast. We have seen earlier that this beast is to be identified with *Rome*, and not with Jerusalem. When this bowl is poured out, the kingdom was filled with darkness. This echoes the judgment that centuries before had fallen upon Egypt, when the darkness was *palpable* (Ex. 10:21-22). We see that these bowls are cumulative in their effect because the people here are still affected by the sores delivered by the first bowl of wrath.

In what way was Rome affected during this time? Jerusalem fell in 70 A.D. but Rome was drastically affected during the same period as well. In fact, there is little doubt that the troubles in Rome provided the defenders of Jerusalem with some of their vain hope. In 69 A.D. Nero was forced to commit suicide, and the scramble that followed is called the "year of the four emperors." Galba, Otho, and Vitellius each successively ruled for a handful of months, and then they were succeeded by Vespasian—who was the general besieging Jerusalem. He returned to Rome, leaving his son Titus to capture the city. These transitions were tumultuous, and in 69 A.D. the great Temple of Jupiter on the Capitoline Hill was burned to the ground—the same fate that would come to Herod's Temple in Jerusalem a very short time later.

What brings repentance is the grace of God. Affliction by itself will never accomplish it. If pain could bring repentance, then Hell would be filled with the penitent. There is a true mystery to lawlessness. These men, afflicted by their sores, covered in darkness, *refused to repent*. They gnawed their tongues in pain, and yet used those same tongues to blaspheme God.

SIXTH BOWL: BEAST AGAINST BEAST

> And the sixth angel poured out his vial upon the great river Euphrates; and the water thereof was dried up, that the way of the kings of the east might be prepared. And I saw three unclean spirits like frogs come out of the mouth of the dragon, and out of the mouth of the beast, and out of the mouth of the false prophet. For they are the spirits of devils, working miracles, which go forth unto the kings of the earth and of the whole world, to gather them to the battle of that great day of God Almighty. Behold, I come as a thief. Blessed is he that watcheth, and keepeth his garments, lest he walk naked, and they see his shame. And he gathered them together into a place called in the Hebrew tongue Armageddon. (Rev. 16:12–16)

We come now to the great battle of Armageddon, the symbolic name for the ultimate defeat of the enemies of God. Many commentators have pointed out that this word served the same way that the battle of *Waterloo* serves us. It refers indirectly to a location, but in general application it means catastrophic defeat.

So the sixth angel pours out his bowl of wrath on the river Euphrates, which was the eastern boundary of the Roman Empire. On the other side of that river was the Parthian Empire. Josephus tells us that the general Titus brought additional reinforcements to the siege of Jerusalem from the region of the Euphrates.

In this vision the waters of the Euphrates were dried up, which provides us with an important scriptural trope. When Daniel interpreted the famous handwriting on the wall for Belshazzar, it was the night before he was killed—Cyrus conquered Babylon that night through the device of diverting the Euphrates, drying it up, and marching into Babylon on the river bed (536 B.C.). In addition, when waters are dried up in Scripture, this indicates a great deliverance for God's people. We saw this in the Red Sea deliverance (Ex. 14:21-22), and in the initial stages of the attack on Jericho (Josh. 3:9-17; 4:22-24). So here the waters of the Euphrates are dried up, opening the way for the "kings of the sunrise" to destroy Jerusalem, which has become the new Babylon.

These armies are gathered through the working of an unholy trinity of three demon-like frogs. This brings to mind the plague of frogs that afflicted Egypt (Ex. 8:1-15)—and remember that Jerusalem has also become the new Egypt

(Rev. 11:8). The fact that the frogs come out of the mouths of the dragon, the beast, and the false prophet indicates that the enemies of God who are going to be destroyed are going to be destroyed by the instrumentality of other enemies of God. In other words, the unbelieving Jews were going to be judged through the pagan Roman armies.

The word Armageddon means Mountain of Meggido, and the location referred to is probably Mount Carmel, where Elijah defeated the priests of Baal. This is the nearest mountain to the plain of Meggido. That battlefield was used more than once—Deborah and Barak achieved their great victory there (Judg. 5:19). The godly king Josiah met his Waterloo there, so to speak (2 Chron. 35:20-25). And so the grim reality represented by this convulsive battle is most likely to be understood as the demolition of Jerusalem.

The Lord here announces that He comes as a thief, which need not refer to His Second Coming. The same phrase was used earlier in Revelation to encourage the saints in Sardis to walk circumspectly (Rev. 3:3). The sixth bowl has been poured out. Very little time is left.

SEVENTH BOWL: REAL HAILSTONES

> And the seventh angel poured out his vial into the air; and there came a great voice out of the temple of heaven, from the throne, saying, It is done. And there were voices, and thunders, and lightnings; and there was a great earthquake, such as was not since men were upon the earth, so mighty an earthquake, and so great.

> And the great city was divided into three parts, and
> the cities of the nations fell: and great Babylon came
> in remembrance before God, to give unto her the cup
> of the wine of the fierceness of his wrath. And every
> island fled away, and the mountains were not found.
> And there fell upon men a great hail out of heaven,
> every stone about the weight of a talent: and men blas-
> phemed God because of the plague of the hail; for the
> plague thereof was exceeding great. (Rev. 16:17–21)

The last of the bowls of wrath is poured into the atmo-
sphere. It is perhaps suggestive that this is described as
the realm of the devil (Eph. 2:2). When this happens, a
great voice comes out from the heavenly temple, crying
out that the judgment is finally complete. As a result there
is a stir and a commotion—voices, thundering, lightning,
culminating in a massive earthquake. There was a great
earthquake, such as had never happened on earth before.

Continuing with our view that these cascading judgments were washing over the city of Jerusalem, we can see
that the cup of wrath she was given to drink corresponds
to the cup of her persecuting sins that is described in the
next chapter. And so given this, it would seem that this
earthquake is the one that was predicted by the prophet
Haggai.

"For thus saith the LORD of hosts; Yet once, it is a little
while, And I will shake the heavens, and the earth, and the
sea, and the dry land" (Hagg. 2:6).

The apostle Paul (as I take the author of Hebrews to be) describes Haggai's prophecy as fulfilled in the destruction of Jerusalem.

> Whose voice then shook the earth: but now he hath promised, saying, Yet once more I shake not the earth only, but also heaven. And this word, Yet once more, signifieth the removing of those things that are shaken, as of things that are made, that those things which cannot be shaken may remain. (Heb. 12:26–27)

As he says in the next verse, we as Christians are receiving a kingdom that cannot be shaken in this way (Heb. 12:28), and the kingdom in its previous form was being taken from the Jews in order to be given to a people who would bear the fruit of it (Matt. 21:43). As John Owen observed, the heavens of their Mosaic worship were being thrown down, and the earth of their political arrangements were being toppled. All was complete, and the stage was set for the transition.[4]

The city was divided into three pieces, which likely was foreshadowed by Ezekiel, and fulfilled in the internecine conflicts between the three factions of the Jewish rebels. The prophet Ezekiel had been told to cut off his hair and to divide it into three portions (Ezek. 5:1-12). This was to represent Jerusalem—"this is Jerusalem" (Ezek. 5:5). A third of the hair was to be burned up, another third was to be slashed with a sword, and the final third was to be thrown to the winds. Ezekiel's dramatic enacted action

---

4. As quoted in Steve Gregg, *Revelation: Four Views* (Nashville, TN: Thomas Nelson, 1997), 392, 394.

referred to the disposal of the inhabitants of Jerusalem in 586 B.C., but it was also a harbinger of the great and final destruction of the city in 70 A.D. And during the siege of Jerusalem (a virtually unconquerable city), the rebels fought against their own interests by fighting with one another—three fierce factions making it possible for the Romans to take the city.

When it comes to the great hailstones, an interesting and suggestive detail is found in Josephus' *Wars* (5.6.3). These hailstones are described as weighing about a talent, which translates into our units of measurement at about a hundred pounds. The Tenth Legion had catapults that could throw these massive stones, which were white. They could throw these things two furlongs or more, which is about a quarter of a mile. Josephus says, "Now, the stones that were cast were the weight of a talent . . . of a white color." Hailstones indeed.

CHAPTER 17

JERUSALEM AS BABYLON

And there came one of the seven angels which had the seven vials, and talked with me, saying unto me, Come hither; I will shew unto thee the judgment of the great whore that sitteth upon many waters: With whom the kings of the earth have committed fornication, and the inhabitants of the earth have been made drunk with the wine of her fornication. So he carried me away in the spirit into the wilderness: and I saw a woman sit upon a scarlet coloured beast, full of names of blasphemy, having seven heads and ten horns. And the woman was arrayed in purple and scarlet colour, and decked with gold and precious stones and pearls, having a golden cup in her hand full of abominations and filthiness of her fornication: And upon her forehead was a name written, MYSTERY, BABYLON THE GREAT, THE MOTHER OF HARLOTS AND ABOMINATIONS OF THE EARTH. And I saw the woman drunken with the blood of the saints, and with the blood of the martyrs of Jesus: and when I saw her, I wondered with great admiration. (Rev. 17:1–6)

After the last bowl had been poured out, one of the angels who had had one of the bowls came to John and talked to him. He said that he would show him the judgment of the great whore, the woman who sat upon many waters.

To help us keep things straight, I will begin with how I identify the figures in this passage. I take the harlot as the apostate city of Jerusalem, the one under judgment. This has been the great theme of the book of Revelation, and it would be odd to change the subject at this late point. I take the beast that she is sitting on as the beast from the sea, introduced to us in chapter thirteen. So I believe we are talking about both Rome and Jerusalem, but Jerusalem as riding upon, dependent upon, the imperial city.

Some reasons for identifying this harlot as Jerusalem can be quickly summarized. The central point of Revelation deals with things that will "shortly" take place (Rev. 1:1). The fall of Jerusalem fits this description, while the fall of Rome occurs centuries later. In terms of literary structure, we are being introduced to the contrast between the harlot and the bride. Because the bride, descending out of Heaven, is the *New* Jerusalem, it stands to reason that the harlot is the Old Jerusalem. Jerusalem is called that "great city" earlier (Rev. 11:8), which is how "Babylon" is described in this section. The use of the word *harlot* fits with the Old Testament usage by the prophets. Harlotry presupposes a covenant relationship with God that was violated by spiritual adulteries (see Is. 1:21; 57:8; Jer. 2:2, 20). And the central charge made against her was that she was guilty of the blood of the prophets, saints, and apostles (Rev. 17:6; 18:20, 24). This was not yet true of Rome, but it had been true of Jerusalem for generations (Matt. 23:35-36).

This said, what are we told in this passage? Instead of being a light to the Gentiles, Jerusalem had led the kings of the earth astray, not to mention the inhabitants of the earth. They all had been made drunk with the wine of her fornication. The angel then led John into the wilderness, a fitting place for a revelation of this nature. It was not a heavenly vision, but rather a vision given in a place of owls and jackals. The woman was sitting on a scarlet colored beast. The color given is new, but in every other respect, the beast is same as before (seven heads, ten horns). The woman riding on the beast is distinct from it, and she was arrayed in scarlet and purple. She was decked out with gold, gems, and pearls, clearly given over to ostentatious and luxurious living. She had a golden cup in her hand, exquisite on the outside, and full of filth on the inside (Matt. 23:25).

She was a wanton, and her name was emblazoned on her forehead. The first thing about her name is that she was a *mystery*. How was it that the people of Israel, delivered by Jehovah so many times, had now come to this? This is the vision that Ezekiel had seen. When God had first seen Israel, she was nothing, polluted in her own blood (Ezek. 16:6). But it was not long before she was seduced by her own beauty (Ezek. 16:14), which was what led to her becoming seductive to everyone else. She was also identified as *Babylon the Great*. We have already considered how that epithet readily applied to Jerusalem, in much the same way that the names of other older pagan entities did—e.g. Sodom and Egypt (Rev. 11:8). She is the *Mother of Harlots*, as well as the *Mother of Abominations on the Earth*.

When John saw her, he was amazed. The woman was regal, clothed in royal splendor, covered in jewelry, but her behavior was that of a slattern. She was *drunk*. Not only was she drunk, but what had made her drunk? She was drunk on the blood of the saints, and on the blood of the martyrs of Jesus. A moment before we had been told that her golden cup was filled with abomination and filthiness of her fornication (v. 4), and earlier it had referred to the wine of her fornication (v. 2). Putting all this together, her abominable lusts appeared to focus on the deaths of the saints—which are precious in the sight of the Lord (Ps. 116:15), and prized by this harlot for a completely different reason.

THE EIGHT HEADS

> And the angel said unto me, Wherefore didst thou marvel? I will tell thee the mystery of the woman, and of the beast that carrieth her, which hath the seven heads and ten horns. The beast that thou sawest was, and is not; and shall ascend out of the bottomless pit,

and go into perdition: and they that dwell on the earth shall wonder, whose names were not written in the book of life from the foundation of the world, when they behold the beast that was, and is not, and yet is. And here is the mind which hath wisdom. The seven heads are seven mountains, on which the woman sitteth. And there are seven kings: five are fallen, and one is, and the other is not yet come; and when he cometh, he must continue a short space. And the beast that was, and is not, even he is the eighth, and is of the seven, and goeth into perdition. (Rev. 17:7–11)

So the angel had shown John a vision of the great harlot, riding on the back of the beast. I believe the simplest way to understand this, as previously explained, is to see the harlot as apostate Judaism and the beast as the Roman Empire. Some additional reasons for taking it this way will unfold as we proceed.

John was amazed at the vision, and the angel asked him why. The mystery of the woman, and the beast carrying her, will be fully explained. The beast in question is the same one that was shown to us earlier in the book—he has seven heads and ten horns. The beast was at one time, is not now, and will ascend out of the Abyss on its way to perdition. On its way to perdition, it will make an impressive display—enough to make all the reprobate on earth wonder. If their names were not written down in the Book of Life (from before the foundation of the world), then they will be the kind of people who are impressed with this kind of thing. The cryptic expression about Rome's reality (was, is not, etc.) is then repeated again, but this time it concludes with a statement about a contrary appearance. The second time John says the beast "was, and is not, and yet is." The beast is finished in principle, but is somehow managing to keep up appearances. And yet is.

John then poses us a riddle, using a similar expression to what he used in chapter thirteen when introducing the mystery of 666. There he said *here is wisdom*, and here he says *here is a mind with wisdom*. It all amounts to the same thing, and is considering the same object.

The beast is identified here two ways—the seven heads of the beast represent seven mountains, and the seven heads of the beast also represent seven kings. The first places the identification as Rome geographically, and the second places it in a particular period of Roman history— the times of the Caesars.

Out of the seven kings, five were already in the history books at the time this vision was given. They were Julius, Augustus, Tiberius, Caligula, and Claudius ("five have fallen"). When John saw this vision, Nero was on the throne ("one is"), and we should also remember that his name can be extracted from John's 666 riddle. The emperor who came after Nero was Galba, and he reigned for only seven months ("continue a short space"). Alternatively, because the time after Nero's death was so tumultuous—a year with three emperors—it could be possible to read the one who continues a very short time as the scramble of all three contenders (Galba, Otho, Vitellius), none of whom were actually firmly *established*.

And this would mean that the indefinite "eighth" would be identified with the Flavian dynasty that followed. Vespasian was the general who was besieging Jerusalem when all this was happening, and as mentioned before, he had to turn over military operations to his son Titus in order go back to Rome and establish order. This Flavian line was Vespasian, Titus, and then Domitian. They are distinct from the seven, and yet like them—like enough to be going to perdition also.

So the woman was riding the beast, but as the prophecy of this book establishes, the beast was going to turn on her. Rome was going to destroy the old Jerusalem, making way for the new Jerusalem.

THE BEAST TURNS ON JERUSALEM

And the ten horns which thou sawest are ten kings, which have received no kingdom as yet; but receive power as kings one hour with the beast. These have one mind, and shall give their power and strength unto the beast. These shall make war with the Lamb, and the Lamb shall overcome them: for he is Lord of lords, and King of kings: and they that are with him are called, and chosen, and faithful. And he saith unto me, The waters which thou sawest, where the whore sitteth, are peoples, and multitudes, and nations, and tongues. And the ten horns which thou sawest upon the beast, these shall hate the whore, and shall make her desolate and naked, and shall eat her flesh, and burn her with fire. For God hath put in their hearts

to fulfil his will, and to agree, and give their kingdom
unto the beast, until the words of God shall be fulfilled. And the woman which thou sawest is that great
city, which reigneth over the kings of the earth. (Rev.
17:12–18)

We turn from the seven heads as seven kings to the question of the ten horns. These ten horns are obviously subordinate to the heads, but they are in some manner kings.
They have real authority, but it is a lesser authority than
that of the seven kings. As it happens, the empire of Rome
did have ten imperial provinces, and it is possible that this
is what is intended. It could also be that the number ten is
symbolic here, simply representing the complete number
of subordinate governors and kings. Scripture itself uses
the term *king* with some latitude—for example, Herod
would be an example of this kind of lesser ruler. His tech-
nical position was that of a tetrarch (which is the term
Luke prefers, e.g. Luke 3:1), but he is also called a king
elsewhere (Matt. 2:1).

The basic set up is this. The waters here are many peoples, nations, tribes, etc. The beast arises from these waters, and the great harlot sits upon the beast. The harlot
thus sits upon the many waters, ruling over them by means
of her dalliance with the beast. The ten horns first make
war on the Lamb, doing so by persecuting His followers.
But the whole thing culminates when Rome turns on the
woman who rides upon its back, thus destroying her. That
said, we can dig into some specifics.

These ten rulers make war on the Lamb and on His followers ineffectually. They do not succeed because the Lord is King of kings and Lord of lords. They inhabit the realm of lower case kings and lords, and thus they are making war on their omnipotent sovereign. It is very specific—"the Lamb shall overcome them." These kings will lose. And those who are with the Lamb are also identified by their calling and character—they are "called, chosen, and faithful." They too are necessarily victorious.

Unable to defeat the Lamb or His people, the kings settle for an entity they can defeat—the harlot. They hate her, and when given the opportunity, they wipe her out. They leave Jerusalem desolate, and naked. They devour her, the ways beasts would eat a carcass, and then burn her with fire. This passage may intend for us to think of Jezebel, eaten at the last by dogs. This is the kind of terrible end that Ezekiel predicted for Israel, and it is now coming to pass.

> Behold, therefore I will gather all thy lovers, with whom thou hast taken pleasure, and all them that thou hast loved, with all them that thou hast hated; I will even gather them round about against thee, and will discover thy nakedness unto them, that they may see all thy nakedness. And I will judge thee, as women that break wedlock and shed blood are judged; and I will give thee blood in fury and jealousy. And I will also give thee into their hand, and they shall throw down thine eminent place, and shall break down thy high places: they shall strip thee also of thy clothes, and shall take thy fair jewels, and leave thee naked

and bare. They shall also bring up a company against thee, and they shall stone thee with stones, and thrust thee through with their swords. And they shall burn thine houses with fire, and execute judgments upon thee in the sight of many women: and I will cause thee to cease from playing the harlot, and thou also shalt give no hire any more. (Ezek. 16:37–41)

These kings are manifestly wicked, and we also see a plain statement of God's absolute control of all such iniquitous rulers. They cannot prevail over the Lord's people, and they will only prevail over their other enemies to the extent that God has determined for them to do so. The text here is as plain as an exegetical pikestaff. *"For God hath put in their hearts to fulfil his will . . ."* Like the ancient Assyrians, they were simply an ax in the hand of a sovereign God (Is. 10:15). They boasted in their prowess, but they had nothing to do *but* fulfill the will of God, and then be condemned for their wickedness in doing so. It was the same as with Herod, Pilate, and Judas, who fell under condemnation for the way that they fulfilled the will of God perfectly (Acts 4:26-28).

The woman was that "great city," who rules over the kings of the earth—until she is destroyed by the kings of the earth. The power of Israel was not a political power. The beast was the political power, and the woman rode on the beast. Her authority, whether corrupt or righteous, was indirect.

There were Jews all over the Roman Empire, and they would all congregate in Jerusalem at the times of festival.

"And there were dwelling at Jerusalem Jews, devout men, out of every nation under heaven" (Acts 2:5). The Jews were God's chosen people, which did not necessarily mean that they were His favorite people. When they trusted and obeyed God, the whole earth was blessed. "And all the earth sought to Solomon, to hear his wisdom, which God had put in his heart" (1 Kings 10:24; cf. Ezra 1:4-7). When they were disobedient, when they fell into unfaithfulness, the Gentile world was stumbled into blasphemy.

> Behold, thou art called a Jew, and restest in the law, and makest thy boast of God, And knowest his will, and approvest the things that are more excellent, being instructed out of the law; And art confident that thou thyself art a guide of the blind, a light of them which are in darkness, An instructor of the foolish, a teacher of babes, which hast the form of knowledge and of the truth in the law. Thou therefore which teachest another, teachest thou not thyself? thou that preachest a man should not steal, dost thou steal? Thou that sayest a man should not commit adultery, dost thou commit adultery? thou that abhorrest idols, dost thou commit sacrilege? Thou that makest thy boast of the law, through breaking the law dishonourest thou God? For the name of God is blasphemed among the Gentiles through you, as it is written. (Rom. 2:17–24)

The Jews were appointed to show the world what blessing for covenantal faithfulness looked like. This meant also, necessarily, that they were appointed to show the world what fierce anger and indignation looks like when

poured out on a virgin bride who became a wanton harlot. This image of harlotry, taken from the Old Testament,
overwhelmingly refers to covenantal apostasy.

So the harlot Jerusalem rode on the back of Rome, but
her position was entirely precarious.

CHAPTER 18

LUXURIOUS JERUSALEM FALLEN

And after these things I saw another angel come down from heaven, having great power; and the earth was lightened with his glory. And he cried mightily with a strong voice, saying, Babylon the great is fallen, is fallen, And is become the habitation of devils, And the hold of every foul spirit, And a cage of every unclean and hateful bird. For all nations have drunk of the wine of the wrath of her fornication, And the kings of the earth have committed fornication with her, And the merchants of the earth are waxed rich through the abundance of her delicacies. (Rev. 18:1–3)

Commentators differ over whether this angel is intended to represent the Lord Jesus, or whether he is simply one of the greater created beings. As there is no explicit reason for identifying him with Christ, it is perhaps best to simply take the description at face value. This is an angel with "great power," and with the kind of vivid luminosity that lit up the earth. The message he declares is one of the great themes of this book—the collapse of the old Babylon, and her replacement by a virgin bride, the new Jerusalem.

The first thing the angel says is that Babylon "the great" has fallen utterly. The first set of descriptions show the greatness of her calamity—and also helps to identify her as the city under judgment, the city of Jerusalem. First, she has become the "habitation of devils" and a stronghold of "every foul spirit." This is precisely what happened to the military defenders of that desolate city, and exactly what Jesus had predicted.

> When the unclean spirit is gone out of a man, he walketh through dry places, seeking rest, and findeth none. Then he saith, I will return into my house from whence I came out; and when he is come, he findeth it empty, swept, and garnished. Then goeth he, and ta- keth with himself seven other spirits more wicked than himself, and they enter in and dwell there: and the last state of that man is worse than the first. *Even so shall it be also unto this wicked generation*. (Matt. 12:43–45)

Jesus was using a cleansed demoniac as an illustration— but what he was actually talking about is what would hap- pen to that unrepentant nation after His ministry of casting out demons. He spent three years casting them out, and yet the rulers of Israel rejected their Messiah. The end result was a revolt against Rome that was literally a pandemonium, a frenzy, a warp spasm of iniquity.

The Lord had said this about Jerusalem—it was going to be flattened.

"And Jesus said unto them, See ye not all these things? verily I say unto you, There shall not be left here one stone upon another, that shall not be thrown down" (Matt. 24:2).

When this kind of complete destruction comes upon a city, the next residents will be the foul and unclean birds. This had been expressly declared as the future of Babylon.

> But wild beasts of the desert shall lie there; And their houses shall be full of doleful creatures; And owls shall dwell there, And satyrs shall dance there. And the wild beasts of the islands shall cry in their desolate houses, And dragons in their pleasant palaces: And her time is near to come, And her days shall not be prolonged. (Is. 13:21–22)

Some question the identification of Babylon here with Jerusalem—was Jerusalem really that great a merchant power, such that the merchants of the earth would weep and lament her fall? I believe that this is the point that John is making—while perhaps he is keying more off the descriptions of an unfaithful and luxury-loving Jerusalem in the Old Testament than he is saying something about the GDP of Jerusalem in the first century. But even here we should be careful—there is no reason for assuming that it was not an economic power.

> Thou hast played the whore also with the Assyrians, because thou wast unsatiable; yea, thou hast played the harlot with them, and yet couldest not be satisfied. Thou hast moreover multiplied thy fornication in the land of Canaan unto Chaldea; and yet thou wast not satisfied herewith. How weak is thine heart, saith the Lord GOD, seeing thou doest all these things, the work of an imperious whorish woman; (Ezekiel 16:28–30, cf. 14-15, 26; 23:12-21)

After all, when we read these words with the assumption that the Old Testament is our primary context, the identification seems sure.

"Babylon hath been a golden cup in the LORD's hand, That made all the earth drunken: The nations have drunken of her wine; Therefore the nations are mad" (Jer. 51:7).

PAID BACK DOUBLE

> And I heard another voice from heaven, saying, Come out of her, my people, That ye be not partakers of her sins, And that ye receive not of her plagues. For her sins have reached unto heaven, And God hath remembered her iniquities. Reward her even as she rewarded you, And double unto her double according to her works: In the cup which she hath filled fill to her double. How much she hath glorified herself, and lived deliciously, So much torment and sorrow give her: For she saith in her heart, I sit a queen, and am no widow, and shall see no sorrow. Therefore shall her plagues come in one day, death, and mourning, and famine;

and she shall be utterly burned with fire: For strong is
the Lord God who judgeth her. (Rev. 18:4–8)

Another voice speaks from Heaven, and summons all of
God's people to "come out from her." This is yet another
indication that the great harlot is the old and fading Judaic
system. It had served its purpose, and because of the great
unfaithfulness and corruption that had grown up among the
leadership of the Jews, God was about to visit a great judgment upon her. And, as follows God's pattern, He calls his
faithful ones away from the catastrophe. He did this with
Noah, He did it with Lot, and Jesus told His followers when
they were supposed to head for the tall grass. "And when ye
shall see Jerusalem compassed with armies, then know that
the desolation thereof is nigh" (Luke 21:20). Then it will be
time to flee to the mountains (v. 21). Jesus even goes so far
as to say that the demolition of Jerusalem will be the culmination of all things. "For these be the days of vengeance,
that all things which are written may be fulfilled" (v. 22).

To remain is to partake of her sins, which means that
such ones would also partake of the judgment.

The cry to come out of Babylon was common in the Old
Testament, and they are worth quoting in a cluster.

Go ye forth of Babylon, flee ye from the Chaldeans,
With a voice of singing declare ye, tell this, Utter it
even to the end of the earth; Say ye, The LORD hath
redeemed his servant Jacob" (Is. 48:20). "Remove out
of the midst of Babylon, and go forth out of the land
of the Chaldeans, And be as the he goats before the
flocks" (Jer. 50:8). "Flee out of the midst of Babylon,

and deliver every man his soul: Be not cut off in her iniquity; For this is the time of the LORD's vengeance; He will render unto her a recompence" (Jer. 51:60). "Deliver thyself, O Zion, that dwellest with the daughter of Babylon" (Zech. 2:7). "Depart ye, depart ye, go ye out from thence, touch no unclean thing; Go ye out of the midst of her; be ye clean, that bear the vessels of the LORD. (Isaiah 52:11)

In short, when the visitation of God finally falls upon apostate Israel, that "Babylon" will not be a good place to be. We want to go out of that city, just as Jesus was taken out of it, and the reproach we will bear will be only temporary. "Let us go forth therefore unto him without the camp, bearing his reproach. For here have we no continuing city, but we seek one to come" (Heb. 13:13–14).

This terrible shakedown of Jerusalem is an indication to us that we are receiving an unshakable kingdom, and so we should be encouraged.

See that ye refuse not him that speaketh. For if they escaped not who refused him that spake on earth, much more shall not we escape, if we turn away from him that speaketh from heaven: Whose voice then shook the earth: but now he hath promised, saying, Yet once more I shake not the earth only, but also heaven. And this word, Yet once more, signifieth the removing of those things that are shaken, as of things that are made, that those things which cannot be shaken may remain. Wherefore we receiving a kingdom which cannot be moved, let us have grace, whereby we may

serve God acceptably with reverence and godly fear:
For our God is a consuming fire. (Heb. 12:25–29)

The sins of Jerusalem had mounted up to Heaven, just as the bricks of Babel had *sought* to rise to Heaven. This ties Jerusalem in with the doomed city of Sodom, another image of judgment from the Old Testament. Jerusalem has already been identified this way (Rev. 11:8), and the fact that her sins have now been noticed is another indication. "I will go down now, and see whether they have done altogether according to the cry of it, which is come unto me; and if not, I will know" (Gen. 18:21).

The fact that the voice from Heaven says that the great harlot will be paid back double is another identifier. In the prophet Jeremiah, it is Israel that will be paid back double for her sins.

And first I will recompense their iniquity *and their sin double*; because they have defiled my land, they have filled mine inheritance with the carcases of their detestable and abominable things. (Jer. 16:18)

Let them be confounded that persecute me, but let not me be confounded: let them be dismayed, but let not me be dismayed: bring upon them the day of evil, *and destroy them with double destruction*. (Jer. 17:18)

Jerusalem as Babylon plays that role completely. Just as Israel was delivered from the Old Babylon, so also the new Israel will be delivered from the New Babylon.

And thou saidst, I shall be a lady for ever: So that thou didst not lay these things to thy heart, Neither didst remember the latter end of it. Therefore hear now this, thou that art given to pleasures, that dwellest carelessly, That sayest in thine heart, I am, and none else beside me; I shall not sit as a widow, neither shall I know the loss of children: But these two things shall come to thee in a moment in one day, The loss of children, and widowhood: They shall come upon thee in their perfection For the multitude of thy sorceries, and for the great abundance of thine enchantments. (Is. 47:7–9)

JERUSALEM GOING DOWN

And the kings of the earth, who have committed fornication and lived deliciously with her, Shall bewail her, and lament for her, When they shall see the smoke of her burning, Standing afar off for the fear of her torment, Saying, Alas, alas, that great city Babylon, that mighty city! For in one hour is thy judgment come. And the merchants of the earth shall weep and mourn over her; For no man buyeth their merchandise any more: The merchandise of gold, and silver, And precious stones, and of pearls, And fine linen, and purple, and silk, and scarlet, And all thyine wood, and all manner vessels of ivory, And all manner vessels of most precious wood, And of brass, and iron, and marble, And cinnamon, and odours, And ointments, and frankincense, And wine, and oil, And fine flour, and wheat, And beasts, and sheep, and horses, and chariots, And slaves, and souls of men. And the fruits that thy soul lusted after are departed from thee, And all things which were dainty and goodly are departed from thee, And thou shalt find them no more at all. The merchants of these things, which were made rich by her, Shall stand afar off for the fear of her torment, Weeping and wailing, And saying, Alas, alas, that great city, That was clothed in fine linen, and purple, and scarlet, And decked with gold, and precious stones, and pearls! For in one hour so great riches is come to nought. And every shipmaster, and all the company in ships, And sailors, and as many as trade by sea, Stood afar off, And cried When they saw the smoke of her burning, saying, What city is like unto this great city! And they cast dust on their heads, And cried, weeping and wailing, saying, Alas, alas, that great city, Wherein were made rich all that had ships in the sea by reason of her costliness! For in one hour is she made desolate. Rejoice over her, thou heaven, And ye holy apostles and prophets; For God hath avenged you on her. And a mighty angel took up a stone like a great millstone, and cast it into the sea, saying, Thus with violence shall that great city Babylon be thrown down, and shall be found no more at all. And the voice of harpers, and musicians, and of pipers, and trumpeters, shall be heard no more at all in thee; And no craftsman, of whatsoever craft he be, shall be found any more in thee; And the sound of a millstone shall be heard no more at all in thee; And the light of a candle shall shine no more at all in thee; And the voice of the bridegroom and of the bride shall be

heard no more at all in thee: For thy merchants were
the great men of the earth; For by thy sorceries were
all nations deceived. And in her was found the blood
of prophets, and of saints, And of all that were slain
upon the earth. (Rev. 18:9–24)

This passage from Revelation 18 consists largely of lists
or inventories of luxury items, and so we will take a larger
section of text all at once. The form of this lament or dirge
is taken from Ezekiel 27-28, where the prophet is offering
up a lamentation for the great merchant city of Tyre. Jerusalem, labeled here as Babylon, has become essentially
pagan in her outlook and is therefore going to receive a
fitting response from God.

Jesus, prophesying the destruction of Jerusalem and the
surrounding nation, compares what was going to happen
to them in the day of judgment to what will happen to
Tyre, and Tyre comes out ahead. "But I say unto you, It
shall be more tolerable for Tyre and Sidon at the day of
judgment, than for you" (Matt. 11:22).

The list of items in vv. 12-13 reads like a luxury cat-
alog—cinnamon and slaves, marble and scarlet. The fact
that the "souls of men" brings up the tail end shows the
dehumanizing effect of all such ostentatious living.

The great image here is that this Babylon will be thrown
into the ocean like a millstone, and will disappear suddenly and rapidly. A similar image can be found in Jeremiah.

And it shall be, when thou hast made an end of reading this book, that thou shalt bind a stone to it, and
cast it into the midst of Euphrates: And thou shalt say,

> Thus shall Babylon sink, and shall not rise from the
> evil that I will bring upon her: and they shall be weary.
> Thus far are the words of Jeremiah. (Jer. 51:63–64).

And here we should once again remember the prophet-ic words of Christ about what would happen to Jerusalem within one generation. The withered fig tree, remember, was a type of fruitless Israel, and a sign of pending judgment.

> And in the morning, as they passed by, they saw the
> fig tree dried up from the roots. And Peter calling to
> remembrance saith unto him, Master, behold, the fig
> tree which thou cursedst is withered away. And Jesus
> answering saith unto them, Have faith in God. For ver-
> ily I say unto you, That whosoever shall say *unto this*
> *mountain*, Be thou removed, and be thou cast into the
> sea; and shall not doubt in his heart, but shall believe
> that those things which he saith shall come to pass; he
> shall have whatsoever he saith. (Mark 11:20–23).

The mountain He was talking about was the mountain He was standing on, and that was yet another image of the looming judgment.

Jerusalem was not the greatest trading center in the world, but it *was* a rich city. What is necessary is for the fall of the city to be a great blow to the merchants and pro-moters, and that certainly happened.

Two other points can be made that help cement the iden-tification of Jerusalem as Babylon headed for the depths.

> Rejoice over her, thou heaven, and ye holy apostles
> and prophets; For God hath avenged you on her . . .

> And in her was found the blood of prophets, and of
> saints, and of all that were slain upon the earth. (Rev.
> 18:20, 24)

This was a city that was guilty of the blood of saints, and prophets and apostles. Sounds like Jerusalem. Jesus had mentioned the blood of Abel and the blood of Zacharias, but it now included the blood of Jesus Himself, and the blood of Stephen and James and numerous others.

> That upon you may come all the righteous blood shed
> upon the earth, from the blood of righteous Abel unto
> the blood of Zacharias son of Barachias, whom ye slew
> between the temple and the altar. (Matthew 23:35)

> Then answered all the people, and said, His blood be
> on us, and on our children. (Matthew 27:25)

And the second thing is that it says in verse twenty that God is rising up to take vengeance for all of it, and this again sounds like Jerusalem.

"For *these be the days of vengeance*, that all things which are written may be fulfilled" (Luke 21:22).

CHAPTER 19

A FELLOW SERVANT

And after these things I heard a great voice of much people in heaven, saying, Alleluia; Salvation, and glory, and honour, and power, unto the Lord our God: For true and righteous are his judgments: for he hath judged the great whore, which did corrupt the earth with her fornication, and hath avenged the blood of his servants at her hand. And again they said, Alleluia. And her smoke rose up for ever and ever. And the four and twenty elders and the four beasts fell down and worshipped God that sat on the throne, saying, Amen; Alleluia. And a voice came out of the throne, saying,

Praise our God, all ye his servants, and ye that fear him, both small and great. And I heard as it were the voice of a great multitude, and as the voice of many waters, and as the voice of mighty thunderings, saying, Alleluia: for the Lord God omnipotent reigneth. Let us be glad and rejoice, and give honour to him: for the marriage of the Lamb is come, and his wife hath made herself ready. And to her was granted that she should be arrayed in fine linen, clean and white: for the fine linen is the righteousness of saints. And he saith unto me, Write, Blessed are they which are called unto the marriage supper of the Lamb. And he saith unto me, These are the true sayings of God. And I fell at his feet to worship him. And he said unto me, See thou do it not: I am thy fellowservant, and of thy brethren that have the testimony of Jesus: worship God: for the testimony of Jesus is the spirit of prophecy. (Rev. 19:1–10)

Just a few verses earlier, a general invitation to rejoice over the destruction of Babylon is issued. This passage sees the invitation received and acted on.

"Rejoice over her, thou heaven, And ye holy apostles and prophets; For God hath avenged you on her" (Rev. 18:20).

The rejoicing begins, and we see the use of the word *Alleluia* four times. This is the only time that this word is used in the New Testament, and it is striking that the occasion for using it is the destruction of Babylon. "Alleluia, the smoke from her ascends forever." Because Babylon is Jerusalem, we see here that her destruction is, in effect, her divorce. Because of her great harlotry, God has finally put her away. And this is why the scene immediately turns to the marriage of Christ to the New Jerusalem. As the New Jerusalem replaces the old Babylon, this makes it clear that the old Babylon is the old Jerusalem.

Salvation, glory, honor and power are given to God for His true and righteous judgments, and these praises are rendered by a "great voice" of many in heaven. The great whore had corrupted the earth with her fornication, and the blood of God's servants was finally and completely avenged. This smoking ruin of a city was by this point not a tragedy, but a cause of great rejoicing. "Alleluia, the smoke from her ascends forever."

As they had done earlier in the book, the elders and the living beasts worshiped the God who sat on the throne, and they added their assent by saying, "Amen. Alleluia."

And then an unidentified voice came out of the throne, and invited all God's servants, everyone who feared, whether small or great, to join in the praise. The invitation is offered to *all* God's servants, and from what happens, it appears that all of them joined in with the praise. A voice like a great multitude responded, a voice like many waters, a voice like multiple thunderings, layered on top of one another, and all together they added the fourth *Alleluia*—the Lord God omnipotent reigns.

The joy was not simply over the removal of corrupt Babylon, but also because it made room for the marriage that was God's intention all along. They said they would be glad and would rejoice, and would give Him honor, because the marriage of the Lamb had come. This is the first indication that we have that the book is going to climax with a wedding. But the bride has known about it because she has spent all this time making herself ready. She did this through her righteous behavior—that behavior was her bridal garment, her white linen.

The angel turned to John, and told him to write out a blessing for those who receive an invitation to this wedding. It is a gloriously mixed metaphor—the saints are the bride, the saints' righteousness makes up the bridal garment, and the saints individually receive invitations to attend the wedding as guests. Those who are invited are blessed, and the angel affirms that these are the true words of God. There was something about this last solemn pronouncement that undid John, and so he fell on his face to worship the angel, who then rebuked him sternly. He said that he must not do that—the angel is just a fellow servant to John, and a fellow servant to anyone else who has the testimony of Jesus. He is told simply to worship God—the testimony of Jesus is the spirit of prophecy.

THE TRIUMPHAL PARADE OF THE CHURCH

And I saw heaven opened, and behold a white horse; and he that sat upon him was called Faithful and True, and in righteousness he doth judge and make war. His eyes were as a flame of fire, and on his head were many crowns; and he had a name written, that no man knew, but he himself. And he was clothed with a vesture dipped in blood: and his name is called The Word of God. And the armies which were in heaven followed him upon white horses, clothed in fine linen, white and clean. And out of his mouth goeth a sharp sword, that with it he should smite the nations: and he shall rule them with a rod of iron: and he treadeth the winepress of the fierceness and wrath of Almighty God. And he hath on his vesture and on his thigh a name written, KING OF KINGS, AND LORD OF LORDS. And I saw an angel standing in the sun; and he cried with a loud voice, saying to all the fowls that fly in the midst of heaven, Come and gather yourselves together unto the supper of the great God; That ye may eat the flesh of kings, and the flesh of captains, and the flesh of mighty men, and the flesh of horses, and of them that sit on them, and the flesh of all men, both free and bond, both small and great. And I saw the beast, and the kings of the earth, and their armies, gathered together to make war against him that sat on the horse, and against his army. And the beast was taken, and with him the false prophet that wrought miracles before him, with which he deceived them that had received the mark of the beast, and them that worshipped his image. These both were cast alive into a lake of fire burning with brimstone. And the remnant were slain with the sword of him that sat upon the horse, which sword proceeded out of his mouth: and all the fowls were filled with their flesh. (Revelation 19:11–21).

Few passages in Revelation enjoy virtually universal agreement from all interpreters—but this is one of them. The rider on the white horse is widely agreed to be Christ Himself. There are three reasons for holding this. First, He is identified as one who is called "Faithful and True." The Lord, the Amen, had spoken earlier in this book at the faithful and true witness (Rev. 3:14). Secondly, He has a self-knowledge that can only be ascribed to God Himself. He had a "name written" which only He Himself knows. This is divine self-knowledge. Redeemed believers have a name that is analogous to this (Rev. 2:17), but that occurs when God gives us a white stone with a name inscribed. It says that only the recipient knows the name, but we may surmise that God also knows—for He is the one who gave the name. In this case, only God knows what God knows. And third, His name is called The Word of God (v. 13; cf. John 1:1). The Word of God *is* God, and the Word of God is *with* God.

In this passage, Christ is coming to "judge and make war." It is commonly (and wrongly) assumed that this is a description of the Second Coming, but there are sound reasons for continuing to believe that this is His fierce judgment on Jerusalem in 70 A.D. The judgment falls on the beast and the false prophet, which we have already identified within the confines of the first century. And we are told that in His Second Coming, the Lord will return the same way that He left—and He did not leave on a horse (Acts 1:11). Here He rides a white horse. Another reason for taking it this way is that the conflict here is driven by the sword that proceeds from Christ's mouth. He is fighting with His Word. It is a spiritual conflict, with very physical results. When Jesus spoke the words of doom forty years before, the fate of Jerusalem was settled. The Word had spoken.

And I might mention in passing that to identify this description erroneously as the Second Coming helps set up the next chapter (in which we find the millennium) with a premillennial understanding. If the Second Coming is in chapter nineteen and the millennium is in chapter twenty, well, there you go.

This judgment is predicted in various ways in a number of places in the Old Testament.

> But with righteousness shall he judge the poor, and reprove with equity for the meek of the earth: And he shall smite the earth with the rod of his mouth, and with the breath of his lips shall he slay the wicked. (Is. 11:4)

> Thou shalt break them with a rod of iron; Thou shalt dash them in pieces like a potter's vessel. (Ps. 2:9)

> Who is this that cometh from Edom, with dyed garments from Bozrah? This that is glorious in his apparel, travelling in the greatness of his strength? I that speak in righteousness, mighty to save. Wherefore art thou red in thine apparel, and thy garments like him that treadeth in the winefat? I have trodden the winepress alone; And of the people there was none with me: For I will tread them in mine anger, And trample them in my fury; And their blood shall be sprinkled upon my garments, and I will stain all my raiment. For the day of vengeance is in mine heart, and the year of my redeemed is come. And I looked, and there was none to help; And I wondered that there was none

to uphold: Therefore mine own arm brought salvation
unto me; And my fury, it upheld me. And I will tread
down the people in mine anger, and make them drunk
in my fury, And I will bring down their strength to the
earth. (Is. 63:1–6)

John is mixing a number of images in an inspired way. In
one place the rod of judgment is what comes from Christ's
mouth, and in another it is His sword. He treads out the
winepress of divine judgment, and Isaiah says that it was
because the "day of vengeance" was in His heart. And in
Luke, the Lord Jesus described what was going to happen
to Jerusalem as the days of vengeance, fulfilling all things.
"For these be the days of vengeance, that all things which
are written may be fulfilled" (Luke 21:22).

I take the army following after Christ here to be glorified saints—but primarily as spectators, not participants.
The Isaiah passage says there was "none to help," and that
there "was none with me." His garments are stained with
blood, and the garments of those who follow Him were
"white and clean." He is the one who trampled out the
grapes of wrath. Another reason for identifying the army
that follows Him with believers (and not angels) is because
of the reference a few chapters earlier (Rev. 14:4). They
follow the Lamb wherever He goes, including here. The
Lord is identified the same way earlier—Lord of lords and
King of kings, and those who are with Him there are the
"called, chosen, and faithful," in short, Christians.

While Christ is the executive of the wrath of God, there
is a sense in which believers participate in the judgment.

He has made us kings and priests (Rev. 1:6; 5:10), and we shall reign on the earth. The rod that comes out of the Lord's mouth is a rod of iron, and it is wielded two ways. One is when He wields it, as in our passage here, but there are places in Revelation where believers participate in wielding that same rod (Rev. 2:26-27).

An angel standing in the sun sets up the great contrast of the final chapters of this vision. We see two banquets—one is the marriage supper of the Lamb (v. 7) and the other is an enormous banquet for carrion birds, and this is also a "supper of the great God" (v. 17). They will feast on kings, on captains, on warriors, on horses, and on the riders of those same horses. They will gorge themselves. And so the armies gathered—the beast and the kings of the earth—and when the fighting was over, the beast was thrown into the lake of fire, along with the false prophet, and anyone who took the mark of the beast, or who had worshiped his image.

Any who remained were slain by the sword of the one who sat on the horse, that is, the Lord Jesus, and the carrion birds were filled.

"He that rejecteth me, and receiveth not my words, hath one that judgeth him: the word that I have spoken, the same shall judge him in the last day" (John 12:48).

CHAPTER 20

THE MILLENNIUM: THE AGE OF THE CHURCH

And I saw an angel come down from heaven, having the key of the bottomless pit and a great chain in his hand. And he laid hold on the dragon, that old serpent, which is the Devil, and Satan, and bound him a thousand years, And cast him into the bottomless pit, and shut him up, and set a seal upon him, that he should deceive the nations no more, till the thousand years should be fulfilled: and after that he must be loosed a little season. (Rev. 20:1–3)

A great angel then descends from Heaven in order to bind the devil. Earlier in the book (Rev. 9:1-3), a star fell to earth, and he was given the key to this Abyss. Because he used the key to open the Pit in order to unleash mayhem on the earth, and given the fact that he is described as *falling* to earth (as opposed to descending), the assumption should be that the earlier star was wicked and rebellious. In contrast, this angel descends in order to lock up the Abyss, and the devil in it. He is not identified here, but given that Michael was the one that successfully fought the devil (Rev. 12:7-8), it may be that we are seeing Michael again here. If Michael threw Satan out of Heaven, it may be that he is the one who also locked him up in the earth.

We can see that we are not talking about a literal physical description from the fact that the devil, a spiritual being, is described as being bound with a chain. This binding is described in particular terms. In other words, the devil is no longer able to deceive the nations in the same way that he had been able to before. Throughout the Old Testament, we see that empires and nations were backed by their gods (e.g. Dan. 10:13, 20; Ezek. 28:11, 14). When nation went to war with nation, their gods were thought to be at war with each other (1 Kings 20:28). The beast, the Roman Empire, was backed in this way by Satan. The devil was the spiritual being that gave the beast its great power. So when he was bound, this meant that he would not be able to prevent the successful evangelization of the Empire, which in fact he was unable to prevent. This was God's plan all along. The Lord Jesus was going to bind the strong man (Mark 3:27), and then take all his stuff. This is one of the reasons for thinking, now that we have come to the twentieth chapter of Revelation, we are looking past the destruction of Jerusalem for the first time. We are promised that when Satan is bound in this way, he will not be able to manipulate the nations the way he was able to before. I do not take this as the vaporization of Satan, but rather as a radical restriction of Satan. Looking at the nations of men, he no longer has the run of the place. Rather, preachers of the gospel have the run of the place, and he can do nothing to stop them.

Our ancient foe is clearly identified for us. He is called the devil here, along with Satan. He is also described in this passage as a dragon, or ancient serpent, which pairs him with the entity which tempted our first parents in the Garden. God had promised the serpent of Genesis that the seed of the woman would trample him underfoot, and this promise comes to fruition when the Roman Christians are told they would crush *Satan* beneath their feet (Rom. 16:20). And John the apostle tells us that the devil was a murderer from the beginning, the one who inspired Cain (1 John 3:8, 12).

Someone has joked that the millennium is a thousand years of peace that Christians like to fight about. It is striking that the major eschatological positions (amillennial, premillennial, and postmillennial) all take their names from a term that shows up in this chapter only, a difficult chapter in a notoriously difficult book. That being the case, I will try to walk through the remainder of this book with some humility, while at the same time trying to be clear about what I believe the book is talking about.

I take the one thousand years of Satan's binding to be a symbolic representation of the Church age, from the time of Pentecost to the Second Coming. The one thousand years represents the fullness and completeness of Christ's reign, not a literal one thousand times around the sun. More about this should become evident as we proceed.

RULING WITH CHRIST

> And I saw thrones, and they sat upon them, and judgment was given unto them: and I saw the souls of them that were beheaded for the witness of Jesus, and for the word of God, and which had not worshipped the beast, neither his image, neither had received his mark upon their foreheads, or in their hands; and they lived and reigned with Christ a thousand years. But the rest of the dead lived not again until the thousand years were finished. This is the first resurrection. Blessed and holy is he that hath part in the first resurrection: on such the second death hath no power, but they shall be priests of God and of Christ, and shall reign with him a thousand years. (Rev. 20:4–6)

And so John saw multiple thrones, which we should understand as being located in Heaven. They are most likely the thrones of the 24 elders, which have already been mentioned (Rev. 4:4). In addition we also see the martyrs, who were assembled earlier under the heavenly altar (Rev. 6:9). In that earlier place, they were crying out for a vengeance that had not yet happened. "How long?" But now that the great blow has fallen, bringing an end to the old

Judaic aeon, these martyrs enter into their share in the rule of the world, in and through Christ. The martyrs are identified as those who refused to participate in the worship of the beast, or of his image, and who refused to accept his mark upon their heads or hands. In this image of their martyrdom, they had been beheaded, which meant that the heads that refused the mark were separated from their bodies—but when that beheading occurred, their heads were unblemished by that particular corruption. They lost their heads, but they were undefiled heads.

Having entered into glory, they continued to live on, and they participated in the reign of Christ over all the nations of men. They are kings and priests together with Him.

What does John mean by "this is the first resurrection"? I believe the best explanation is that the first resurrection is the resurrection of Jesus Christ, and the second resurrection is the general resurrection of the dead at the end of all human history. John's expression in v. 6 points toward this understanding. The first resurrection is something that we are blessed to "have part" of. Christ rose from the dead as the first fruits of those who had died (1 Cor. 15:20)—His resurrection was the firstfruits *for others*. In another place, He is described as being the firstborn from among the dead (Col. 1:18)—again, His resurrection was a resurrection that others were to participate in. When we are converted, by faith we are made partakers of Christ's death, burial, *and resurrection*. He was raised to life for our justification (Rom. 4:25). "For if we have been planted together in the likeness of his death, we shall be also in the likeness of his resurrection" (Rom. 6:5). If we are baptized, we are baptized into His death, and it is not possible to be baptized into His death without participating in "newness of life" (Rom 6:4).

John also adds the detail that the "rest of the dead" would not be raised until the thousand years, which is the Christian aeon, was completed. I take this as referring to the resurrection of the unjust, the resurrection of the unbelievers. That there is such a resurrection is plain in Scripture.

> And have hope toward God, which they themselves also allow, that there shall be a resurrection of the dead, both of the just and unjust. (Acts 24:15)

> Marvel not at this: for the hour is coming, in the which all that are in the graves shall hear his voice, And shall come forth; they that have done good, unto the resurrection of life; and they that have done evil, unto the resurrection of damnation. (John 5:28–29)

So every believer who is truly converted throughout all church history is made a partaker of the resurrection of Jesus, the first resurrection. The second death has no power over them—which means they can look forward to the general resurrection as a great hope. In addition, they are included in the reign of Christ over the nations, which is taught in multiple other places. For just one example, consider this: "And hath raised us up together, and made us sit together in heavenly places in Christ Jesus" (Eph. 2:6). And so the shared rule with Christ is *not* limited to first century martyrs. It applies to every believer who trusts in Christ at any point in the millennium.

There is no need to take the reference to this millennium, this one thousand years, as a literal one. This is a symbolic number, in a symbolic chapter, in a highly symbolic book. Throughout Scripture, it is used as a place holder for a very large number—the number of hills where God owns the cattle (Ps. 50:10), the number of enemy soldiers that one Israelite will pursue (Josh. 23:10), and the number of generations with whom God keeps covenant (Deut. 7:9). And references to a thousand years are also obviously figurative. "For a thousand years in thy sight are but as yesterday when it is past, and as a watch in the night" (Ps. 90:4; cf. Eccl. 6:6, 2 Pet. 3:8).

THE OUTCOME NOT IN DOUBT

> And when the thousand years are expired, Satan shall be loosed out of his prison, And shall go out to deceive the nations which are in the four quarters of the earth, Gog and Magog, to gather them together to battle: the number of whom is as the sand of the sea. And they went up on the breadth of the earth, and compassed the camp of the saints about, and the beloved city: and fire came down from God out of heaven, and devoured them. And the devil that deceived them was cast into the lake of fire and brimstone, where the beast and the false prophet are, and shall be tormented day and night for ever and ever. (Rev. 20:7–10)

Just a few verses before, we were told that Satan was locked up in the Abyss such that he would no longer be able to "deceive the nations." That this was the nature of his restriction is reinforced here—when he is released from his prison at the end of the thousand years, he goes out and resumes his lying activities. Once again, he deceives the nations.

So at the very end of the long period of Christian ascendancy, Satan is permitted to lead the nations astray again. The nations involved are described as being at the "four quarters of the earth," meaning all the nations hither and yon. The name given to them is taken from Ezekiel 38 and 39. In Ezekiel, this referred to an unbelieving and savage nation from the north. The prophecy there is against Gog, the prince of that people, and Magog, the people themselves. When they attacked Israel (in overwhelming numbers), they were nevertheless defeated. Thus they serve as a fitting type for this international version of the same kind of thing. One time the old Israel was assaulted by Magog, and Magog was overthrown. And here, the new Israel is assaulted by an international Magogian confederacy, and they too are thrown down immediately.

Satan's deception was initially successful, in that he was able to gather an army like the "sand of the sea." One question might be why God allows for something like this after the world was successfully evangelized. The best explanation appears to be that He is showing us that salvation is all of grace. After centuries of gospel glory, it would be easy for men to start taking credit for what the gospel alone accomplished, and so God illustrates for us the fact that apart from grace, the human heart remains exactly what it has always been—by nature an object of wrath.

So after a long period of gospel glory, Satan is permitted one last attack on the object of his malice, which is the Christian church. This is pictured by two images—the "camp of the saints" and the "beloved city." The camp of the saints brings the period of the wilderness to mind, and the beloved city is talking about the New Jerusalem, the Christian Church. Both descriptions are of God's beloved people, the apple of His eye. Because the church of the faithful will at that point be located all over the earth, we see the enemies of God going up "on the breadth of the earth." Christians will be attacked in the same way that the Jews were attacked by Haman in the Persian empire—attacked, that is, in every town, every city, every province, and every nation.

But the outcome of this attack is not in doubt. This is an attempted murder, not a murder. The faithful are surrounded, and so they have a full opportunity to trust the Lord. But the Lord will defend His people, and will rain down fire on the enemies of God. I don't believe there is any reason to assume the fire here is merely figurative. "In flaming fire taking vengeance on them that know not God, and that obey not the gospel of our Lord Jesus Christ" (2 Thess. 1:8). I take this destruction of Satan, and of "Gog," and of "Magog," as the Second Coming of Christ.

The beast and the false prophet had been thrown into the lake of fire, the final death, sometime earlier. Now Satan is consigned there—no longer in the Abyss, he is now in final death. In that place, he is tormented day and night forever and ever. This is as good a place as any to mention that Satan is not the king of Hell. Jesus is the ruler of Hell, and Satan is in torment there.

"In that day the LORD with his sore and great and strong sword shall punish leviathan the piercing serpent, even leviathan that crooked serpent; and he shall slay the dragon that is in the sea" (Is. 27:1).

DEATH AND HADES CAST OUT

> And I saw a great white throne, and him that sat on it, from whose face the earth and the heaven fled away; and there was found no place for them. And I saw the dead, small and great, stand before God; and the books were opened: and another book was opened, which is the book of life: and the dead were judged out of those things which were written in the books, according to their works. And the sea gave up the dead which were in it; and death and hell delivered up the dead which were in them: and they were judged every man according to their works. And death and hell were cast into the lake of fire. This is the second death. And whosoever was not found written in the book of life was cast into the lake of fire. (Rev. 20:11–15)

And so John saw a great white throne, upon which Christ is seated in glorious splendor. We know that Christ is the one on the throne because of the numerous ways Scripture indicates this. Christ was earlier associated with a white cloud (Rev. 14:14), and he was seen riding on a white horse (Rev. 6:2; 19:11). Here it is fitting that He is established as Judge on a white throne.

More to the point, this scene is obviously the last judgment ("the earth and the heaven fled away"), and the Bible is explicit that Christ is the one who will rule at that judgment. For example, Christ has the authority to "execute judgment" (John 5:27).

> When the Son of man shall come in his glory, and all the holy angels with him, *then shall he sit upon the throne* of his glory. (Matt. 25:31)

> I charge thee therefore before God, and the Lord Jesus Christ, *who shall judge* the quick and the dead at his appearing and his kingdom. (2 Tim. 4:1)

> He that rejecteth me, and receiveth not my words, hath one that judgeth him: the word that I have spoken, *the same shall judge him in the last day.* (John 12:48)

> Because he hath appointed a day, in the which *he will judge the world in righteousness* by that man whom he hath ordained; whereof he hath given assurance unto all men, in that he hath raised him from the dead. (Acts 17:31)

So this is the final judgment, and we have a contrast—between one book on the one side, and "the books" on the other. That one book is the Book of Life, and the one specific thing we are told about it is that it contains a list of names.

Notwithstanding in this rejoice not, that the spirits are subject unto you; but rather rejoice, because *your names are written in heaven.* (Luke 10:20)

To the general assembly and church of the firstborn, *which are written in heaven* . . . (Heb. 12:23)

He that overcometh, the same shall be clothed in white raiment; and *I will not blot out his name out of the book of life*, but I will confess his name before my Father, and before his angels. (Rev. 3:5)

So the issue here is simple and binary. Either your name is in the Book of Life, or it is not. If a person's name is *not* in the Book of Life, then he is judged in accordance with the other books, and these other books are histories, detailed biographies. These people are judged "according to their works," which is repeated twice, in both verses 12 and 13. Anyone whose name was not found in the Book of Life was cast into the lake of fire, with the degree of punishment a function of the works they had done or left undone.

The sea gave up her dead, and so also both Death and Hades gave up their dead. This is the resurrection of the unjust. Earlier we saw that through His resurrection from the dead Christ came into possession of the keys of both Death and Hades (Rev. 1:18). He is the ultimate conqueror, and now in this final triumphant act, He throws both Death and Hades into the lake of fire. This indicates, incidentally, that Hades was a place for departed shades, a temporary place of judgment, until the time should come for that judgment to be made permanent. Death and Hades were thrown into the final death, the second death, the lake of fire, or Gehenna.

CHAPTER 21

THE NEW JERUSALEM

And I saw a new heaven and a new earth: for the first
heaven and the first earth were passed away; and
there was no more sea. And I John saw the holy city,
new Jerusalem, coming down from God out of heaven,
prepared as a bride adorned for her husband. And I
heard a great voice out of heaven saying, Behold, the
tabernacle of God is with men, and he will dwell with
them, and they shall be his people, and God himself
shall be with them, and be their God. And God shall
wipe away all tears from their eyes; and there shall
be no more death, neither sorrow, nor crying, neither

shall there be any more pain: for the former things are passed away. And he that sat upon the throne said, Behold, I make all things new. And he said unto me, Write: for these words are true and faithful. And he said unto me, It is done. I am Alpha and Omega, the beginning and the end. I will give unto him that is athirst of the fountain of the water of life freely. He that overcometh shall inherit all things; and I will be his God, and he shall be my son. But the fearful, and unbelieving, and the abominable, and murderers, and whoremongers, and sorcerers, and idolaters, and all liars, shall have their part in the lake which burneth with fire and brimstone: which is the second death. (Rev. 21:1–8)

There are four basic approaches to interpreting the book of Revelation. One of them is the *futurist*, which regards the events predicted as being fulfilled overwhelmingly in *our* future. The second is the *idealist* approach, which takes the book as something of a cosmic parable, with no specific earthly fulfillments. The third is the *historicist*, which takes the fulfillment of the prophecies as an unfolding reality, down through all of church history. The last, and the approach that has been taken throughout this commentary, is the *preterist*. This comes from the Latin word for past, and means that the prophecies given were fulfilled in the prophet's future, but in *our* past—and for the most part overwhelmingly in the first century.

I mention this because we are now in the part of the book where such clean distinctions are hard to maintain.

In the previous chapter, we saw the Second Coming (*futurist*), and in these last two chapters we see a *historicist* description of all of church history, as the New Jerusalem descends. I would simply encourage everyone to sit loose in the saddle, and to maintain a sense of humor.

We are seeing here the transition between the first heaven and first earth (the Judaic aeon) and the new heaven and new earth (the Christian aeon). For various reasons, I do *not* take the new heaven and new earth as referring to the post-Second Coming eternal state. The first is that the prediction of the new heaven and earth comes from the prophet Isaiah, and he describes it for us.

> For, behold, I create new heavens and a new earth:
> And the former shall not be remembered, nor come
> into mind. . . . There shall be no more thence an infant
> of days, Nor an old man that hath not filled his days:
> For the child shall die an hundred years old; But the
> sinner being an hundred years old shall be accursed.
> (Is. 65:17, 20)

What do people do in the new heavens and new earth? Well, among other things, they die. That will not be the case after the Second Coming.

Secondly, Peter talks about Isaiah's prophecy as something that was right on top of his readers, and Jude apparently interprets him that way also. And when Jude refers to those who "separate themselves," he has particular faces in mind.

> Nevertheless we, according to his promise, *look for new heavens and a new earth*, wherein dwelleth righteousness. (2 Peter 3:13)

> But, beloved, remember ye the words which were spoken before of the apostles of our Lord Jesus Christ; how that they told you there should be mockers *in the last time*, who should walk after their own ungodly lusts. These be they who separate themselves, sensual, having not the Spirit. (Jude 17–19)

So I take the first heavens and earth as the Judaic aeon and the new heavens and earth as the Christian aeon, and these two aeons overlapped—the latter beginning at Pentecost, and the former ending with the destruction of the Temple in 70 A.D. The destruction of that Temple has been one of the major themes of this book of Revelation.

So the New Jerusalem is the bride of Christ, which is explicitly stated in the next section (v. 9), which means that she is the Christian Church. Church history is the time it takes for this bride to walk down the aisle. By the time she gets to the front of the cathedral, she will be without spot or wrinkle or any other blemish (Eph. 5:27). When she arrives at that final destination, then all sorrow will have been banished, and there will never again be any more tears.

As she is descending out of Heaven, a great voice declares that the *tabernacle* of God is now with men. The Church is the Temple of the Holy Spirit, and this is how it is possible for God to dwell with men and for every form of sorrow to be sponged away.

The process of world evangelization is the process by which God is making all things new, which is the declaration He makes in this passage. The old world order is passing away (1 John 2:17), so that the new order may be established on the firm foundation of the Word of God. For the Christian, all things have become new (2 Cor. 5:17).

It is striking that the one who sits upon the throne here (Christ) says the same thing that He said from the cross. It is finished (John 19:30). When Babylon, the evil city was destroyed, a loud cry from the Temple said that it was "done" (Rev. 16:17). And here, again, it is said that it is "done" (Rev. 21:6).

And so, as Christ's bride is working through her wedding prep, as she is adorning herself for that great and final day of consummation, she needs to remember that all of church history is nothing but wedding prep. Her bridegroom, the Alpha and Omega, summons her. He is the beginning and the end, the whole point of all history. He promises living water to anyone who thirsts, and shows us His tender care for His people. He promised this to the Samaritan woman at the well (John 4:10, 14), and later He gives the invitation at a great Jewish festival (John 7:37ff). He speaks the same word here.

The one who overcomes will inherit everything, and this characteristic promise reminds us of how He spoke to the seven churches at the beginning of the vision. And a somber note is also struck, when we are reminded that this is to be a holy bride, and so excluded from her are all vile lovers of vile living. One harlot has already been put away and judged for such things, and so they have no place with the new bride who is preparing herself.

NEW TEMPLE

> And there came unto me one of the seven angels which had the seven vials full of the seven last plagues, and talked with me, saying, Come hither, I will shew thee the bride, the Lamb's wife. And he carried me away in the spirit to a great and high mountain, and shewed me that great city, the holy Jerusalem, descending out of heaven from God, Having the glory of God: and her light was like unto a stone most precious, even like a jasper stone, clear as crystal; And had a wall great and high, and had twelve gates, and at the gates twelve angels, and names written thereon, which are the names of the twelve tribes of the children of Israel: On the east three gates; on the north three gates; on the south three gates; and on the west three gates. And the wall of the city had twelve foundations, and in them the names of the twelve apostles of the Lamb. And he that talked with me had a golden reed to measure the city, and the gates thereof, and the wall thereof. And the city lieth foursquare, and the length is as large as the breadth: and he measured the city with the reed, twelve thousand furlongs. The length and the breadth and the height of it are equal. And he measured the wall thereof, an hundred and forty and four cubits, according to the measure of a man, that is, of the angel. And the building of the wall of it was of jasper: and

the city was pure gold, like unto clear glass. And the
foundations of the wall of the city were garnished with
all manner of precious stones. The first foundation was
jasper; the second, sapphire; the third, a chalcedony;
the fourth, an emerald; The fifth, sardonyx; the sixth,
sardius; the seventh, chrysolite; the eighth, beryl; the
ninth, a topaz; the tenth, a chrysoprasus; the eleventh,
a jacinth; the twelfth, an amethyst. And the twelve
gates were twelve pearls; every several gate was of
one pearl: and the street of the city was pure gold, as
it were transparent glass. (Rev. 21:9–21)

The New Jerusalem descending from Heaven to earth is a
glorious vision of the Christian church. But before considering the details of the symbolism, we should reinforce the
point that it is symbolism. The city is described as being a
perfect cube—with each side being 1200 stadia, which cal-
culated into a modern measurement is about 1500 miles.
If this were to be taken as a literal city, if it landed, its base
could cover over half of the United States with its eastern
base covering Baltimore, and its western base barely missing Denver. Then because the city is as tall as it is wide,
it would be sticking 1500 miles up into space, knocking a
goodly number of satellites out of the sky. On top of that,
in each 1500 miles stretch along the base, there are three
gates, 12 in all. Each gate is made out of a single pearl.
The gates are enormous, and each one is fashioned from
one pearl. If literal, then God apparently has an oceanic
planet somewhere with some giant oysters. We are better
off looking for the meaning that these symbols bring to us.

One other thing should be mentioned briefly. Many of our popular tropes for Heaven come from this passage (pearly gates, streets of gold), but John is revealing the nature of the *Church* to us, not the nature of Heaven. This is not a symbol of the afterlife, but rather a symbol for the bride of Christ.

There is a strong juxtaposition between this virgin bride and the great harlot. In both places, John is taken in the Spirit to a particular place to be shown a woman. In both places, an angel prefaces it with *come, I will show you*. In this vision, John is carried in the Spirit to a great and high mountain, where he is shown the bride. Earlier in Revelation (17:1), he is taken in the Spirit into the wilderness (17:3), to be shown the judgment of the harlot. We are given to understand that both women are beautiful, but one in a pure way and the other in a corrupt and decadent way. The New Zion is beautiful for situation (Ps. 48:2). The angel who shows John this glorious vision was one of the angels who had poured out one of the bowls full of wrath—indicating that God's purposes of wrath and mercy are ultimately one.

Both are priest's daughters, but this New Zion is a worthy daughter. The old Jerusalem is burned with fire because she played the whore in her father's house.

> And the ten horns which thou sawest upon the beast, these shall hate the whore, and shall make her desolate and naked, and shall eat her flesh, and burn her with fire. (Rev. 17:16)

> And the daughter of any priest, if she profane herself
> by playing the whore, she profaneth her father: she
> shall be burnt with fire. (Lev. 21:9)

The bridal dress for the New Jerusalem is the Shekinah Glory. She is described as "having the glory of God" (v. 11). In a sense, all of church history should be understood as us yearning for that dress, yearning to be adorned with that glory (Rom. 2:7; Rom. 5:2; Rom. 8:18; Col. 1:27, and many others).

Remember that Paul teaches us elsewhere that the Christian church is built on the cornerstone of Christ Jesus, and on the foundation stones of the apostles and prophets (Eph. 2:20). We have the same image here in the description of this great city. There are twelve gates, and each gate has the name of one of Israel's tribes inscribed (v. 12). There are twelve foundation stones, and on them were the names of the twelves apostles (v. 14). There was an angel at each gate, and each angel is associated with a particular tribe. This lends support to the idea that the angel of the churches in the early chapters were human messengers, human "angels."

> Then they that feared the LORD spake often one to
> another: And the LORD hearkened, and heard it, And
> a book of remembrance was written before him For
> them that feared the LORD, and that thought upon his
> name. And they shall be mine, saith the LORD of hosts,
> In that day when I make up my jewels; And I will spare
> them, as a man spareth his own son that serveth him.
> (Mal. 3:16–17)

The city has great walls, walls that are 144 cubits tall. These walls are the walls called Salvation, and they run all the way around the base of this towering skyscraper of a city.

"Violence shall no more be heard in thy land, Wasting nor destruction within thy borders; But thou shalt call thy walls Salvation, and thy gates Praise" (Isaiah 60:18).

The gates are called *Praise,* which is the meaning of the name of the tribe of Judah. Judah is the tribe through whom the Christ came, and so we should understand Judah as representing all Israel, which is why John mentions that each tribe is associated with a gate.

The foundation stones that are the apostles are not limestone or granite. They are represented by means of an array of precious stones. We are not told which apostle goes with which precious stone, but there appears to be a meaning in how John arranges it. Predicting the church, the prophet Isaiah says this:

"O thou afflicted, tossed with tempest, and not comforted, behold, I will lay thy stones with fair colours, and lay thy foundations with sapphires. And I will make thy windows of agates, and thy gates of carbuncles, *and all thy borders of pleasant stones*" (Isaiah 54:11–12).

Isaiah's gemstones and those in Revelation vary, but John appears to have a point to the order he presents them. These are the precious stones associated with the signs of the zodiac—but John lists them in reverse order.

The fact that there are three gates facing each direction of the compass is a wonderful picture of the universal offer of the gospel. Three gates are facing in each direction, and all men everywhere are summoned to move to this city. We see elsewhere in Scripture that this is exactly what they do, streaming in from every direction.

"And they shall come from the east, and from the west, and from the north, and from the south, and shall sit down in the kingdom of God" (Luke 13:29).

This city is expressly identified as the church, the bride of Christ (Rev. 21:9). The Jerusalem above, Paul says, is the mother of us all (Gal. 4:26). The mother of individual Christians is the bride of Christ collectively. As mentioned earlier, the city is a cube, which is the same shape as the Holy of Holies, which is another way of referring to the Christian church. You are the Temple of the Holy Spirit, Paul says (1 Cor. 3:16-17; 1 Cor. 6:19).

NEW HOLY OF HOLIES

And I saw no temple therein: for the Lord God Almighty and the Lamb are the temple of it. And the city had no need of the sun, neither of the moon, to shine in it: for the glory of God did lighten it, and the Lamb is the light thereof. And the nations of them which are saved shall walk in the light of it: and the kings of the earth do bring their glory and honour into it. And the gates of it shall not be shut at all by day: for there shall be no night there. And they shall bring the glory and honour of the nations into it. And there shall in no wise enter into it any thing that defileth, neither whatsoever worketh abomination, or maketh a lie: but they which are written in the Lamb's book of life. (Rev. 21:22–27)

Remember that the New Jerusalem is the Christian Church. This new city contains no temple because the Father and *Son* are the Temple, and the entire city is the body of the Son. The Christian Church is the Holy of Holies, and so the city is the Temple. No sun is necessary, and no moon, because it is lit by the glory of God. As the Israelites had the Shekinah glory to accompany them by night and day, so also the saints of God have the glory of God that lightens their way. The Lamb Himself is the light of the city—"Then spake Jesus again unto them, saying, *I am the light of the world*: he that followeth me shall not walk in darkness, but shall have the light of life" (John 8:12). The Lamb is the light of the city, and the nations that are saved shall walk in the light provided by Him. The kings of the earth—distinct from the city—bring their glory and honor into the city. In other words, the nations of men do homage to the church. The city is unthreatened, with the gates never shut. The gates are not shut during the day, and it is always day, never night. John then repeats the fact that the glory and honor of the nations is brought into the church. Nothing enters the church that would defiled her—no one who does abominable things, or who fashions a lie. The only ones who enter are those who are written in the Lamb's Book of Life, meaning the elect.

Throughout this passage, John is riffing off the Isaianic vision. The New Jerusalem is illuminated by the glory of God alone (v. 23). And Isaiah says this: "The sun shall be no more thy light by day; Neither for brightness shall the moon give light unto thee: But the LORD shall be unto thee an everlasting light, and thy God thy glory" (Is. 60:19).

This city shall be a light of the world; the nations of men will stream to it. The nations of the saved will walk in the light provided by the city. And Isaiah says this same thing: "And the Gentiles shall come to thy light, and kings to the brightness of thy rising" (Is. 60:3).

The kings of the earth bring their glory and honor to her; the nations of men bring their honor and glory to the city of God. And Isaiah says the same thing. "And their kings shall minister unto thee . . ." (Is. 60:10). "And that their kings may be brought . . ." (Is. 60:11) "The glory of Lebanon shall come unto thee . . ." (Is. 60:13).

The gates of the New Jerusalem shall not be shut during the day, and it is always day. This is basically what Isaiah foretold: "Therefore thy gates shall be open continually; they shall not be shut day nor night . . ." (Is. 60:11).

John repeats himself when he says that the Gentile nations will bring their glory to the church. Isaiah repeats the point as well. "Then thou shalt see, and flow together, and thine heart shall fear, and be enlarged; Because the abundance of the sea shall be converted unto thee, the forces of the Gentiles shall come unto thee" (Is. 60:5).

No one is permitted to track in anything that defiles. No sin will be scraped off on the golden streets. Isaiah had a vision for this kind of holiness as well. "Thy people also shall be all righteous: They shall inherit the land for ever, The branch of my planting, the work of my hands, that I may be glorified" (Is. 60:21). Note it well. The people will all be *righteous*.

Arise, shine; for thy light is come, And the glory of the LORD is risen upon thee. For, behold, the darkness shall cover the earth, And gross darkness the people: But the LORD shall arise upon thee, And his glory shall be seen upon thee. And the Gentiles shall come to thy light, And kings to the brightness of thy rising. (Is. 60:1–3)

CHAPTER 22

NO NIGHT THERE

And he shewed me a pure river of water of life, clear as crystal, proceeding out of the throne of God and of the Lamb. In the midst of the street of it, and on either side of the river, was there the tree of life, which bare twelve manner of fruits, and yielded her fruit every month: and the leaves of the tree were for the healing of the nations. And there shall be no more curse: but the throne of God and of the Lamb shall be in it; and his servants shall serve him: And they shall see his face; and his name shall be in their foreheads. And there shall be no night there; and they need no candle, neither light of the sun; for the Lord God giveth them light: and they shall reign for ever and ever. (Rev. 22:1–5)

There is a pure river there, filled with the water of life, clear as crystal. This river flows from the throne of God, which is also the throne of the Lamb. Comparing this passage with the something that the Lord says in the gospel of John, we see that this river is the Holy Spirit, flowing not only from the throne of God, but also from the hearts of all believers.

In the last day, that great day of the feast, Jesus stood and cried, saying, If any man thirst, let him come unto me, and drink. He that believeth on me, as the scripture hath said, *out of his belly shall flow rivers of living water. (But this spake he of the Spirit,* which they that believe on him should receive: for the Holy Ghost was not yet given; because that Jesus was not yet glorified.) (John 7:37–39)

This makes good sense because the holy city Jerusalem is a symbol of that great body of believers.

This particular vision that John passes on to us draws on at least three Old Testament prophets.

And it shall be in that day, *that living waters shall go out from Jerusalem;* half of them toward the former sea, and half of them toward the hinder sea: in summer and in winter shall it be. (Zech. 14:8)

> And it shall come to pass in that day, that the mountains
> shall drop down new wine, and the hills shall flow with
> milk, and all the rivers of Judah shall flow with waters,
> and a fountain shall come forth of the house of the LORD,
> And shall water the valley of Shittim. (Joel 3:18)

In the form of the vision that Ezekiel gives us, this living
water flows out of the Temple, over the threshold, and gets
deeper and deeper as it goes (Ezek. 47:1-5).

The tree of life lines both sides of the river, indicating
that the tree of life is a *kind* of tree. There are multiple
trees. This kind of tree is able to produce a different crop
of a different kind of fruit on a monthly basis. Not only so,
but the leaves of these trees are of use in healing the nations. Ezekiel had seen the same glorious reality.

> Now when I had returned, behold, at the bank of the
> river were very many trees on the one side and on the
> other. (Ezek. 47:7)

> And by the river upon the bank thereof, on this side
> and on that side, shall grow all trees for meat, whose
> leaf shall not fade, neither shall the fruit thereof be
> consumed: it shall bring forth new fruit according to
> his months, because their waters they issued out of the
> sanctuary: and the fruit thereof shall be for meat, and
> the leaf thereof for medicine. (Ezek. 47:12)

As this glorious city advances toward the culmination of
her blessing, which would be the final day of resurrection,
we see at that point that the curse that had been laid on

our world at the beginning (Gen. 3:15ff) is finally undone. There shall be "no more curse." The reason that there is no longer any curse is because the throne of God, the throne of the Lamb, is in it. God's servants will serve Him truly.

We see that this would appear to indicate the full number of the elect. These are the servants of God who are privileged to "see His face." "Blessed are the pure in heart: for they shall see God" (Matt. 5:8).

In addition to this, His name is on their forehead. This in turn helps us identify the 144,000 as a symbol of all the elect, all the saved—for this is what was said about them earlier: "And I looked, and, lo, a Lamb stood on the mount Sion, and with him an hundred forty and four thousand, *having his Father's name written in their foreheads*" (Rev. 14:1). And earlier than that, in chapter seven, after John had *heard* the number of 144,000 (Rev. 7:4), he then *looked* and saw a multitude that no one could count (Rev. 7:9). He heard the number, and then saw the innumerable multitude.

John then repeats what was said in the previous chapter. There is no night there—there is constant light coming from the Lord God. There is no artificial light needed there either. And the inhabitants of the New Jerusalem shall reign forever and ever.

THE UNSEALED PROPHECY

And he said unto me, These sayings are faithful and true: and the Lord God of the holy prophets sent his angel to shew unto his servants the things which must shortly be done. Behold, I come quickly: blessed is he that keepeth the sayings of the prophecy of this book. And I John saw these things, and heard them. And when I had heard and seen, I fell down to worship before the feet of the angel which shewed me these things. Then saith he unto me, See thou do it not: for I am thy fellowservant, and of thy brethren the prophets, and of them which keep the sayings of this book: worship God. And he saith unto me, Seal not the sayings of the prophecy of this book: for the time is at hand. (Rev. 22:6–10)

The book of Revelation has an epilogue, which begins here and continues through to the end of the vision. One of the angels who poured out one of the bowls of wrath is continuing to speak to John. He speaks words that are "faithful and true," and here the angel is repeating an assurance which God Himself had spoken from His throne in the previous chapter (Rev. 21:5). God is identified by this angel as being the "Lord God of the holy prophets," which seals for us something that has been obvious throughout the entire book of Revelation. The vision that John gives us is a vision that has been *saturated* in Old Testament prophecies. The Lord revealed here really is the Lord God of the holy prophets.

One of the great neglected themes of the book is that the Lord is coming quickly. This is *not* the same thing as saying that when He comes, whenever that is, it will be sudden. John has been telling us from the first verse on that these are things that must "shortly come to pass" (Rev. 1:1). Here he says that the Lord's angel was sent in order to reveal to His servants what must "shortly be done" (Rev. 22:7).

The word is the same in both instances (*taxos*)—the events predicted were barreling down on the denizens of the first century, and were overwhelmingly fulfilled at that time.

Another argument in favor of this conclusion can be derived from the fact that John is told something very different from what Daniel was told.

"But thou, O Daniel, shut up the words, and seal the book, even to the time of the end: many shall run to and fro, and knowledge shall be increased" (Daniel 12:4).

Daniel was told to seal up the words of his prophecy because it was going to be a while yet. This means that Daniel was told to seal up his prophecy for events that were not going to come to pass for another four centuries. So what sense would it make for John to be told not to seal up the words of his prophecy for events that would be 20 centuries or more in coming to pass? So not only does John not seal his words, but he also (in effect) *unseals* the words of Daniel, which were all coming to fruition at this same time—along with many glorious prophecies throughout the rest of the Old Testament Scriptures. The Lord God *of the holy prophets* had sent this vision.

This passage contains the sixth blessing that is given in the course of the book—"blessed is he that keepeth the sayings of the prophecy of this book." For all intents and purposes, this is the same blessing that the book began with. Not only so, but let us emphasize once again the reason why there is a blessing for the one who reads, and who hears, and who keeps the things that are written.

"Blessed is he that readeth, and they that hear the words of this prophecy, and keep those things which are written therein: *for the time is at hand*" (Rev. 1:3).

The angel who communicates all of this to John must have been an angel of great glory and magnificence because John makes the same mistake again (vv. 8-9), the mistake of attempting to worship a fellow creature, and a fellow servant of all who keep the sayings of this prophecy the way they should.

"And I fell at his feet to worship him. And he said unto me, See thou do it not: I am thy fellowservant, and of thy brethren that have the testimony of Jesus: worship God: for the testimony of Jesus is the spirit of prophecy" (Rev. 19:10).

OUTSIDE THE CITY

> He that is unjust, let him be unjust still: and he which is filthy, let him be filthy still: and he that is righteous, let him be righteous still: and he that is holy, let him be holy still. And, behold, I come quickly; and my reward is with me, to give every man according as his work shall be. I am Alpha and Omega, the beginning and the end, the first and the last. Blessed are they that do his commandments, that they may have right to the tree of life, and may enter in through the gates into the city. For without are dogs, and sorcerers, and whoremongers, and murderers, and idolaters, and whosoever loveth and maketh a lie. (Rev. 22:11–15)

The massive judgments outlined in this book are imminent. A final appeal for repentance is given in the form of
saying that there is no real time for repentance. The one
who is unjust might as well stay that way. The one who is
filthy . . . let him be filthy still (v. 11). The same thing goes
for the righteous and holy. That all this is tied to the near-
ness of the disasters is seen in the next phrase—"behold, I
come *quickly*" (v. 12). Telling the filthy and the unjust that
there is no time might stir them up to act while there is still
(almost) time.

The Lord is coming quickly, and He has every man's
paycheck in hand. Every man will have the response of
God apportioned in accordance with his work. This theme
comes up in Scripture again and again (Matt. 16:27;
25:31ff; Rom. 2:6; 1 Pet. 1:17; Rev. 20:13). This in no way
conflicts with our salvation being all of grace, and entirely
apart from works, as we can see in the arguments that Paul
makes. The book of Romans is all about salvation by grace
through faith, and yet one of the texts cited above is from
early on in Romans. And we see how grace and works har-
monize in his words elsewhere.

"For by grace are ye saved through faith; and that not
of yourselves: it is the gift of God: Not of works, lest any
man should boast. For we are his workmanship, created
in Christ Jesus unto good works, which God hath before
ordained that we should walk in them" (Eph. 2:8–10).

We have been saved by grace through faith, and not of
works. No man has any cause for boasting. We are not
saved by good works, but we are in fact saved to good
works. We are created in Christ Jesus to good works, works

that were ordained beforehand for us to walk in. As fore-
ordained works, this means that they necessarily follow
salvation by grace. And, as such, there is no inconsistency
when God uses them as an infallible indicator that salvation by grace has in fact occurred.

Another passage that highlights the consistency of grace
and works is this one:

> Wherefore, my beloved, as ye have always obeyed, not
> as in my presence only, but now much more in my
> absence, work out your own salvation with fear and
> trembling. For it is God which worketh in you both to
> will and to do of his good pleasure. (Phil. 2:12–13)

We are to work out our salvation, but this is only possible as we are working out what God is working in. And so
it is that we are saved by works—the work of Christ on the
cross, and the works of the Spirit within us, which works
are, from our perspective, entirely and utterly gracious.

All the glory goes to Christ, who is the Alpha and Omega, the beginning and end, and the first and last (v. 13). All
the reprobate are judged by their works, and their wages
are nothing but justice. All the saints are judged by the
white linen of their righteous deeds, and are received into
glory, and together they join their voices to praise the one
who gave them that white linen. All their robes were cut
from one bolt of cloth, and that cloth is the entire possession of Jesus Christ, and those with whom He shares it.

The seventh and last benediction in this book is then
given. Blessed are those who do His commandments (v.
14). Keeping the commandments of God is itself a gift and

grace, and those who walk in God's ways are permitted to walk up to the tree of life and partake of it. Those who walk in His ways are permitted to come through the gates of the glorious city. They have free access to the City of God, being full citizens of it.

Excluded from the City (in this last and glorified state) are the evil-doers. The first category mentioned is that of *dogs*. There are various possibilities here. One is that Jews formerly used this term to describe the Gentiles, but this would be odd now since we have just seen John describing the glory and honor of the nations (*ethnoi*, Gentiles) streaming into the City (Rev. 21:26). Another usage is where Paul turns the epithet around, and applies it to the Judaizers (Phil. 3:2). This is possible, but given the nature of the other sins listed, it seems out of place. The last possibility, and the most likely one, is that it is referring to homosexuals.

"Thou shalt not bring the hire of a whore, or the price of a dog, into the house of the Lord thy God for any vow: for even both these are abomination unto the Lord thy God" (Deut. 23:18).

This is referring to a male homosexual prostitute, and it is telling that the prohibition is banning the profits of such activity from being brought into the "house of God." This is the same kind of context that John is talking about. So who is excluded? Who may not come in to defile the translucent city? Outside are the dogs, the witches, the pimps and johns, the abortionists and other murderers, those who bow down before senseless images, and whoever loves a lie, and loves to make them up.

THE INVITATION

> I Jesus have sent mine angel to testify unto you these things in the churches. I am the root and the off-spring of David, and the bright and morning star. And the Spirit and the bride say, Come. And let him that heareth say, Come. And let him that is athirst come. And whosoever will, let him take the water of life free-ly. (Rev. 22:16–17)

Jesus famously asked the Jews how David could have called the Messiah Lord when the Messiah was to be descended from David (Matt. 22:42, 45). How could a Davidson be someone that David himself would bow down to? We have the same issue here. Jesus had sent His angel to testify to the churches all the contents of this book, and here at the conclusion, He says "I am the root and the offspring of David." He is the root of David, the one from whom David arose, and he is also the offspring of David, the one who descended from the line of David.

In addition, Jesus claims that He Himself is the bright and morning star. This morning star was the planet Venus, often visible as the last of the stars in the morning. He had promised the saints in Thyatira that He would give them the morning star (Rev. 2:28), which means that He will give them Himself. Peter had used the same imagery when he said that the hope of believers would be realized when the day dawns, and the morning star would arise in their hearts (2 Pet. 1:19).

An invitation to come is then issued, and it is worth asking to whom the invitation is directed. Is it a prayer for the Lord Jesus to come? He had promised a short time before to "come quickly" (vv. 7, 12). And right after this, John prays that the Lord would come quickly (v. 20). It would be easy to assume that this is making the same point. But this appears to be a different invitation—an invitation to the one who is thirsty. The one who desires to partake of the water of life is invited to come and drink from the water of life. This appears to be an evangelistic invitation. The Spirit issues the invitation, and the bride of Christ gives the same invitation. Furthermore, the one who hears the words of this book adds his *Amen* to it.

COME, LORD JESUS

> For I testify unto every man that heareth the words of the prophecy of this book, If any man shall add unto these things, God shall add unto him the plagues that are written in this book: And if any man shall take away from the words of the book of this prophecy, God shall take away his part out of the book of life, and out of the holy city, and from the things which are written in this book. He which testifieth these things saith, Surely I come quickly. Amen. Even so, come, Lord Jesus. The grace of our Lord Jesus Christ be with you all. Amen. (Rev. 22:18–21)

Because the book of Revelation is the last book in the Bible, and because many have come to think of it as one single book, instead of being a library of 66 books, not a few have taken this final malediction to be referring to anyone who messes around with the contents of Scripture. No doubt that is *also* a bad thing to do, but the curse that is stated here is a curse that applies to the contents of the book of Revelation itself. The reference is to "this book," and a particular feature of the Apocalypse—all the plagues of the book—are specifically mentioned and applied.

Now what is true of the parts also happens to be true of the whole. If someone ought not tamper with the book of Revelation, it would not be good to tamper with the books that came before. This is a scriptural way of thinking.

> Ye shall not add unto the word which I command you, neither shall ye diminish ought from it, that ye may keep the commandments of the Lord your God which I command you. (Deut. 4:2)

> What thing soever I command you, observe to do it: thou shalt not add thereto, nor diminish from it. (Deut. 12:32)

> Add thou not unto his words, Lest he reprove thee, and thou be found a liar. (Prov. 30:6)

The malediction is for those who adjust the content of the Scriptures to suit themselves. It should not be applied to those who disagree with us about the precise meaning of the seventh bowl of wrath.

If a person supplements this revelation with his own thoughts, then God will supplement him with all the plagues mentioned. If someone takes away from this revelation on the basis of his own wisdom, then God will take away his portion of the Book of Life, and his portion in the holy city, and from the things (e.g. blessings) that are mentioned in this book. This does not mean that someone can be removed from God's roster of the elect. But it *does* mean removal from the covenanted and visible church, and all the blessings that pertain to it.

The one who testifies to these things—that is, the Lord Jesus—says that He is coming quickly. John responds with a heartfelt invitation—even so, come, Lord Jesus. And the book concludes with a simple but glorious benediction. The grace of our Lord Jesus Christ be with you all. Amen.

And Amen.

CAN'T TELL THE PLAYERS WITHOUT A SCORECARD

Revelation is a big book, with a lot of different symbols and characters. To help you in case you have trouble keeping track of things, here is a list of various characters and significant symbols in Revelation and what I think they represent.

144,000: The elect

2 Witnesses: The prophets

4 Riders: Christus Victor, bloodshed, famine, and a combination of sword, famine, pestilence, and wild animals

4 Beasts: Cherubim

666: The numerical value of Neron Caesar

7 Lampstands: Seven churches of Asia

7 Spirits: The Holy Spirit

7 Stars: Seven pastors of the churches of Asia

24 Elders: The Elect, specifically the twelve tribes of Israel (the Old Covenant) and the twelve apostles of the church (the New Covenant)

Babylon/Harlot: Jerusalem

Beast of the Land: Priesthood of Israel in cahoots with Rome

Beast of the Sea: The Roman Empire

Mark of the Beast: Emperor-worship

New Jerusalem/Virgin Bride: Christian Church, purified from sin

Seal on the Forehead: The exodus of Christians from Jerusalem

Sodom/Egypt: Jerusalem

Woman and her offspring: The faithful remnant of Israel with the converted Gentile Church